Praise for *Turn Your Life Around*

"Dr. Tim Clinton deals not only with the reality of brokenness but the great possibility of restoration with compassion and practicality. In TURN YOUR LIFE AROUND, biblical principles become tools that anyone can use to follow the path of recovery to a place of lasting victory. A must-read for those struggling to recover from personal setbacks or those seeking to encourage the wounded."

—Michelle McKinney Hammond, author of
Release the Pain, Embrace the Joy

"Tim Clinton is a genius at personal relationships. His own family is a shining example of love in action. He shares his heart and soul in his new book, TURN YOUR LIFE AROUND. Don't miss this heartwarming and practical look at how to make the most out of your future in spite of your past."

—Dr. Jerry Falwell, founder/chancellor/president of
Liberty University, Lynchburg, Virginia

"When you're hurting, confused, or stuck in a place you don't want to be, what you long for is a way to turn things around. This book is what you or a hurting friend has been looking for: a positive, encouraging way of escape from past hurts, and practical guidance toward God's best."

—John Trent, PhD, president, The Center for Strong Families

"Bothered by life stressors and robbed by insidious dependencies, many warriors have lost their effectiveness for Christ. Through encouragement and spiritual guidance, Tim Clinton offers a way back in this informative new book, TURN YOUR LIFE AROUND." Frank Minirth, MD

"Tim Clinton has been strategically positioned by God to reach a broad audience with a transforming message. This book may just be his magnum opus. It's written from a heart consumed with Christ to hearts longing to break free into the reality of God's power and plan."

—Larry Crabb, NewWay Ministries

continued . . .

"There is no more devastating experience to a pastor or a leader of people than to see someone who seemed to have it all together emotionally and spiritually suddenly take a nosedive into self-destruction, self-pity, and futility. Think what it must be like for that person. In TURN YOUR LIFE AROUND, Tim Clinton provides both pastors and those who struggle a road map for a return trip to wholeness—a trip only God can orchestrate."

—H. B. London Jr., vice president, Church, Clergy
and Medical Review, Focus on the Family

"Every comeback starts with a defining moment. No matter what's happened, what you've done, or where you've been, you can change your life; and TURN YOUR LIFE AROUND tells you how. This book by Dr. Tim Clinton will trigger your spiritual transformation."

—Dr. Tony Evans, senior pastor, Oak Cliff Bible Fellowship;
president, The Urban Alternative

"Tim Clinton has a clear understanding of the human condition and of the suffering, the fears, and the bondage under which people live. His heart of compassion and his utter confidence in the transforming power of God to heal and redeem are evident throughout this book. It will instill hope both for yourself and for suffering humanity."

—Diane Langberg, PhD, psychologist

"Pain and adversity can easily tempt us into superficial service to God instead of true relationship with God. He has our brains but not our hearts. This book leads us back from our distracting activities to our 'first love'—true intimacy with God."

—Dr. Michael Lyles, psychiatrist, Lyles and
Crawford Consulting, Atlanta, GA

TURN
YOUR LIFE
AROUND

Break Free from Your Past
to a New and Better You

Dr. TIM CLINTON

Faith Words™

New York　Boston　Nashville

FaithWords
Hachette Book Group USA
237 Park Avenue
New York, NY 10017

Visit our Web site at www.faithwords.com.

Printed in the United States of America

First Edition: November 2006

10   9   8   7   6   5   4   3   2

FaithWords is a division of Hachette Book Group USA, Inc.
The FaithWords name and logo is a trademark of Hachette Book Group USA, Inc.

Library of Congress Cataloging-in-Publication Data
Clinton, Timothy E., 1960–
Turn your life around : break free from your past to a new and better you / Tim Clinton. — 1st FaithWords ed.
       p.   cm.
Summary: "Noted counselor Tim Clinton explains the key to being able to turn our lives around by understanding how God uses our sense of powerlessness to draw those who are hurting back to him"—Provided by the publisher.
   ISBN 978-0-446-57910-0
1. Providence and government of God.   2. God—Omnipotence.
3. Consolation.   4. Suffering.   5. Hope—Religious aspects—Christianity.
I. Title.
   BT135.C55   2006
   248.4—dc22

2006007539

To my brothers and sisters, with whom
I have shared so much joy in life:
Joy Calvert, James Clinton, Ruthann Smulik,
Gale Smulik, Candace Mayersky, Tom Clinton,
and Wendy Wagner.

CONTENTS

Part II: Recovery of Heart: Coming Out of Pain

ACKNOWLEDGMENTS

No book is ever published from the work of one author; it takes many dedicated persons. Therefore, it is very humbling to have my name alone on the cover of this book when so many others have contributed to the work you hold in your hands right now. Many thanks are in order.

Foremost I would like to thank Larry Walker for his diligence in assisting with the writing of this book. I love your passion for Christ and life. Similarly, both Dr. Anthony Centore and Joshua Straub put in many long hours and worked in tandem with Larry and me. Both contributed significantly to the research and editing.

A special thank-you goes to Tom Winters, my agent, who stepped up and believed in this work from the first mention and introduced me to the wonderful publishing team at FaithWords, especially Chip McGregor and Holly Halverson.

I'd also like to acknowledge the many mentors, teachers, and fellow Christians who have walked with me and taught me about life over the last twenty years or more. In particular, I would like to thank Drs. Diane Langberg, Ron Hawkins, Michael Lyles, Archibald Hart, and Larry Crabb: your wisdom and kindness have always been felt.

Also, to Dr. John Ortberg, whom I have referenced extensively: your lectures at AACC events are an inspiration to me and to our members.

Thank you to my friend and colleague Dr. Gary Sibcy: your research and our mutual work on attachment relationships is foundational to the process of regaining heart.

To Jimmy Queen, Troy Morgan, and George Ohlschlager: your excitement about this book and its potential was the energy I needed to finish and get this work to press.

Many thanks to the executive board and each staff member of the AACC. The fruit of your work has resulted in changed lives all across the globe. The same is true for our AACC members: it is an honor to serve you, and you never cease to amaze.

Some brave persons allowed me to tell their stories in this book. Their names, identities, and aspects of their stories have been modified to assure absolute anonymity. If you think you recognize someone in this work, I am absolutely certain you are mistaken.

Finally, I would err greatly not to thank my intelligent and beautiful wife, Julie, and our two wonderful children, Megan and Zach. The three of you have sacrificed more than anyone and you deserve deep love. God has been so kind to us, and I love every moment of life with you.

FOREWORD

In all my years of ministry, I have taught that God's Word is sufficient for every situation in life. No matter how devastating or horrific circumstances may seem, God has provided instruction in His Word on what to do particularly in times of pressure and crisis. God promises us that He will supply all of our needs (Phil. 4:19).

Satan would like nothing better than to see us spin our wheels while in the pit of our mistakes and hurts, rendering us useless for God's kingdom. The success of Satan's plan is that we get caught up in our circumstances instead of going to the Word of God for instruction.

Tim Clinton understands the major issues facing people today. His training in biblical psychology and careful study of God's Word have brought him to discover new ways to use

God's Word to solve the problems of life. Tim and I share the benefit of being mentored in Christian counseling by the great Dr. Henry Brandt, the first secular-trained psychologist to bring biblical principles to the counseling room.

Dr. Brandt always agreed with the apostle Paul when he said, "No temptation has overtaken you except such as is common to man; but God is faithful, who will not allow you to be tempted beyond what you are able, but with the temptation will also make the way of escape, that you may be able to bear it" (1 Cor. 10:13). The Bible indeed has the answers to the problems of life.

My prayer would be that the reading of this book creates healthy individuals who are inspired to "work heartily unto the Lord."

—Dr. Tim LaHaye
Author and Pastor

INTRODUCTION

It is for freedom that Christ has set us free.

Galatians 5:1 NIV

People get hurt, frustrated, and discouraged for a number of reasons. Some people create their own troubles through wrong decisions and actions. Many people suffer at the hands of others or simply because of circumstances beyond their control. I wrote this book primarily for those who are facing tough times through no fault of their own—good people who love and walk with God until the wounds of life turn them away.

Life can be pretty unmerciful. Loss of a loved one, loss of a job, a financial challenge or ruin, betrayal, a bad marriage, an illness like cancer: all involve that sick feeling inside that life is not the way it is supposed to be. When it isn't, we instinctively work to recover what we lost. If the answers don't come quickly, stomachs start to turn, ulcers bleed, tempers flare, and the wounds begin to go deep into the soul.

Our normal reactions to life's *ambush* on the soul and its destructive *assault* on our bodies, marriages, and relationships can get ugly fast. Either we get *angry*, or we fall victim to a gnawing *anxiety* that drives us deep into the shadow lands of fear. We shouldn't blame anybody for his or her initial reactions to these attacks.

The downward spiral from assault and ambush to anger and anxiety happens to both good and bad people alike. We are all susceptible to this overwhelming journey into the abyss of pain.

When our pain continues to go unresolved, a heaviness begins to envelop our lives, leaving us feeling terribly *alone* and *alienated* from man and God.

As we feel more and more isolated from others, we are often perceived as *arrogant* and uncaring, but our hearts are blinded by pain. Sometimes we walk away from God because we are past feeling anything good.

This disaffection with God leads to dangerous diversions and flirtations with experiences, things, or relationships that seem to dull our pain—what I call *adulteries of the heart*. Finally, we begin to descend even more on our journey into *addiction*—diversions and flirtations become fixed and compulsive idols, false gods we cling to in our pain and desperation. Any remembrance of our original pure devotion to Christ seems to be light-years away. Evil whispers lies to immobilize us, diluting our hope for a better life.

As we plummet toward the bottom, we may even lose heart and begin to doubt the character of God Himself.

The good news is that God is always at work to win our hearts. He loves to use our brokenness and powerlessness to send us fleeing back to Him.

There *is* a path to healing if you will cast your eyes on the Lover of your soul! New beginnings start with an understanding of what has happened each step of the way on the downward spiral. Your natural tendency will be to bypass the effort to understand your pain and instead focus on recovery. But *you can't heal what you can't see or feel.*

I want to take you on a journey. It's a journey during which you're going to have to be brutally honest with yourself. It may be uncomfortable—you might see pieces of yourself that you don't like. No matter how difficult, hold on to hope because there is *healing* in this journey! By understanding the process and path of brokenness, you begin to heal. If you can understand the *why* of your wounds, then the *how* of coming out of your pain will begin to make sense.

Jesus described a prodigal son who experienced the defining moment of his life when he "came to his senses" one day and said, "I will get up and go to my father" (Luke 15:17–18 NASB). If you are hurting, you may not want to admit it. But if you'll take that first bold step, your life journey will take you in a completely new direction.

When you shelter your heart and hide behind the pain through denial, the lack of honest evaluation of what happened in your life can leave you feeling empty and exhausted, yet yearning for more. No matter how bad life seems at the moment, I'm gambling that you are gutsy enough to take a good look into your soul. Once you do, you can begin to look up. And *that* is when you will catch your first glimpse of a new life!

This healing path, this upward spiral to hope and recovery of heart, begins to make sense only as you realize your sheer dependence on God and how desperately you need to be rooted in His *affection* for you. This sets the stage for an important *assessment* of the practices and behaviors in life that you need to purge, and those you need to plug in.

As you look inward, a greater level of self-*awareness* takes place, opening the door for true intimacy with—*attachment to*—God and others. As the intimacy grows, your life begins to produce the fruit of godly *action* bathed in *accountability* and the essence of feeling *alive again!*

This is the journey toward healing and wholeness, and it is nothing less than a marvelous work of God.

I long to take every hurting and wounded person I meet on the remarkable journey to recovery revealed in these pages. The more I go through it, the more passionate I am about it. As a professional counselor and instructor of counselors, I've waded through and produced my own share of counseling material. But I've never done anything like this! This is not merely a book for your head; it is a book of hope for the heart. I crafted it for everyone who longs to live out a dream and fulfill the deepest cries of the heart.

If you or someone you love is suffering, then set your course to rediscover and reclaim life the way it was really meant to be!

This journey will radically alter the way you approach an intimate relationship with God and with those you love, especially your spouse, your children, and your parents. It will even change the way you look at ministers and the ministry and will transform your friendships.

Finally, it will free you to deliver living messages of hope to others so they in turn can be free too. This much we know: only God can set the soul free! No counselor can do that. All hell is against your success, but more importantly, all of heaven is devoted to your success! I'm praying for freedom and victory in your life.

When you finally recover your heart, then you are literally alive again, and the destroyer is defeated in your life. From that moment, you can begin to savor every moment of life and maximize every opportunity in Christ.

Such is God's dream for our lives, a place where the great accuser is overcome and a new and better life is won. Do you want to be free? Do you want to see others released to pursue their destinies? Then I invite you to read on!

Turn Your Life Around

· PART I ·

Losing Heart:
The Descent into Pain

· 1 ·

AMBUSHED AND ASSAULTED
Coping with the Unexpected

Life is no fun when things aren't the way they are supposed to be.

How do you live with someone who seemingly doesn't love you? How do you love someone who misuses and abuses you? It hurts to be rejected, blamed, or unjustly accused.

How do you go on when you feel all alone, when life leaves you feeling bruised, beaten, and as if you're going nowhere?

How do you parent children who think you are the worst thing that ever happened to them?

How do you cope with all of the things that compete for and against what you love and hold dear?

Why do normally sensible people abandon all hope for what should have been their blessings in Christ?

What force or elemental power is sucking the life and tearing the hearts right out of us?

Wherever you look, you'll find the eight out of every ten people who aren't living out their dreams.[1] Most of them are simply worn down. They have surrendered their hopes and traded their dreams for the uniform of uniformity. They have forgotten or simply never understood God's promise of the abundant life (John 10:10).

This darkness that threatens the hearts and faith of good people is nothing less than an *ambush of the heart*! The assault often begins with a major disappointment or sorrow that wages war on the mind and the soul. An attack may begin in quiet ways, creeping in on the back of chronic exhaustion with a nagging suspicion that we lack something other people seem to have in abundance.

We don't want to admit the attack exists or acknowledge that it affects us. It is easier to revert to our favorite childhood solution: if we whistle in the dark loud and long enough, perhaps our nagging, secret fear—the unnamed specter that traces our steps day and night—*will just go away*!

✦ *The assault is too deadly to ignore or dismiss.*

This silent shadow seems able to break us down and inspire fear and heartbreaking hopelessness without warning. Perhaps it is the reason behind the treason of Peter in the garden when he denied Jesus. Could this help explain why the once-loving husband and dad meets another woman for lunch at the local bar across town? Is this a dark influence drawing the beloved Sunday school teacher to the adult bookstore night after night?

The assault is too deadly to ignore or dismiss. Someone far

wiser than I once explained that "heartache crushes the spirit" (Prov. 15:13 NIV). Today, hard-won experience—suffering—has made me quick to confirm the wisdom of these ancient words.

A Divine Encounter in a Bar

We serve a good and loving God, but in His wisdom He seems to allow things to drop into our laps that shake us to the core. This is exactly how God ignited the fire in me that birthed this book. I'll never forget the divine appointment that diverted me from my scheduled meeting in a restaurant.

I had to walk through a bar area to reach the business luncheon in the back of a restaurant. As I did so, I glanced at the bartender's extremely long beard. (My generation would instantly recognize its similarity to the trademark beards of ZZ Top, an old rock-and-roll band from the 1970s.)

I chuckled and kept walking until I thought about the man's eyes. Something about the man's face seemed familiar. Then it hit me—I knew this bartender. This was a man who had invested in my personal and spiritual life several years earlier. What was he doing behind a bar?

Moved in my spirit, I turned around and walked straight back to him. (Although I'm a Christian and a licensed professional counselor, I'm still known for being a little crazy on occasion.) I bellied up to the bar, crossed my arms, and waited for the bartender to notice me. It didn't take long.

I looked at him and he looked at me. Then I said, "Hey," and he said, "Hey." Once the introductions were over, I tried to zero in and gently ask, "What's up? What are you doing here?"

He said, "I'm getting my stuff together, *that's* what I'm doing!" (Except he didn't say "stuff.")

I stood silent and he could tell I was still inquisitive in my mind.

"To explain would take more than you've got time for," he said. After that we made small talk and before long, I turned and walked away. I prayed, "Lord, what takes a man like him from fresh faith—a place of closeness with You—to a place like this?"

This was a good man, a very good man, who had taught me about relationships and foundational Scriptures such as: "If any man be in Christ, he is a new creature" (2 Cor. 5:17 KJV) and "Ye are bought with a price: therefore glorify God in your body" (1 Cor. 6:20 KJV). He thought he was getting his life together, but it was obvious he was as lost as a baseball in high weeds. What had happened to him? How did he lose the power he once had in his life? Even more, what is the pathway of recovery? How do people really break free to new life? Or do they?

People are hurting! And the pain is *not* merely limited to the unsaved masses. Something is seriously wrong in Christian City, and God is ready to fix it. But how?

. . . So began the thinking that led to this book.

Widespread Hurt

Far too few of us seem willing to admit there is a problem. From my perspective, this is the sad part. We sing boldly in our church buildings, but little evidence of our personal pain ever leaks out into the streets, the homes, or the cities around us. Who or what has silenced the lambs of God? Why are we so afraid to admit our failures and heartbreaks?

The fact is, "church people" divorce just as often as people who never attend church—in fact, multiple divorces are extraordinarily common among born-again Christians; 23 percent are divorced two or more times![2] Some consider our most serious social ill the lack of fathers in the home. This fatherless trend harms our emerging younger generation and promotes mental disorders, crime, suicide, poverty, teenaged pregnancy, drug and alcohol abuse, and incarceration.[3] Nearly three of every four children living in fatherless homes experience poverty right now, and they are ten times as likely to experience extreme poverty.[4] (And that is only a measure of their status as financial have-nots. The void in their souls defies calculation.)

I don't mean in any way to slam single parenting. If anything, I applaud and marvel at single parents who work so hard to give the gift of love to their kids. But the fact remains that no mom is a mom-dad. And no dad can be a dad-mom.

✦ *Even our heroes are hurting,*
and no one but God seems to be listening!

We are more stressed than ever before, we're pulled in every direction, we don't have time for anything. Add to that dismal picture the fact that hell itself is against us. Verses such as 1 Peter 5:8 confirm this fact: "Your enemy the devil prowls around like a roaring lion looking for someone to devour." None of us is exempt.

Good people are hurting. Even our heroes are hurting, and no one but God seems to be listening! A group of about thirty missionaries came to me and we talked for two hours. I walked out of that meeting with pain in my heart. We had talked about what it meant to be a missionary and they told me things that I had never heard.

One man stood up at the end and said, "Tim, I guess what

we want to know most of all is that we matter. We want to know that what we do really counts." (This came from missionaries who had dedicated their entire lives to foreign ministry!)

What sobered me was the fact that they had given so much. It is true that they had heaven's reward, and none of them worked for the accolades of man. But they had endured great stress and sacrifice. They just needed to be reassured that it was worth it. Do you ever feel this way?

✦ *It is time to claim our freedom from the accuser.*

Those God Uses Are Especially at Risk

I am a pastor's son. I know firsthand what service looks like: I've seen my father go through distress and weep over his congregation. In my ministry as a professional counselor, I've seen great pastors struggling with deep sin in their lives. I've helped them cope with the aftermath of treachery and stood alongside them as they went through brokenness in their ministry.

You may be one of the pastors or full-time ministry workers who know what I'm talking about. You may even be one of the 40 percent of pastors who'd like to leave the pulpit.[5] Apparently, when asked why, these spiritual leaders said they just didn't want to do it anymore. I can understand why. It seems the office of pastor doesn't mean much today. It is not an easy job, and it's often not fun.

My friend H. B. London, the man often called "America's pastor to pastors," once said, "We have found that most members of the clergy feel isolated, insecure, and only rarely affirmed."[6]

But whether you are a pastor or a different servant of God,

you and I are in an all-out battle against disaffection with God and life. It is time to claim our freedom from the accuser.

Regardless of our occupations or life journeys, we *all* face spiraling stress levels and increasing satanic assault. The Bible itself warns us that in the last days, evil will grow worse and worse.

✦ *The enemy appears to be putting in some overtime*
before quitting time.

The enemy knows direct assault usually won't work against genuine, born-again Christians, so he most often uses schemes or guerrilla warfare tactics against us. He attacks around the edges of our lives, targeting our children, our spouses, our thought lives, our health, or our finances. Although we don't want to give him too much credit, he is a serious student of human behavior.

He knows that if he can get to your marriage, then he can get to you. And he also knows that if he successfully compromises your marriage, he can profoundly influence your kids and ultimately influence or weaken the church.

On top of everything else, he is getting impatient. Look at Revelation 12:12: "Woe to the inhabitants of the earth and of the sea! For the devil is come down unto you, having great wrath, because he knoweth that he hath but a short time" (Rev. 12:12 KJV). He appears to be putting in some overtime before quitting time.

We *do* have God's promises and His ability to see us through anything and everything. But when your courage flags, my focus is to help you through those moments spent on the brink, at the edge of despair and human frailty. The problem isn't your immediate response; it is how you deal with the attack in the long run. Your choices determine your future.

✦ *Your choices determine your future.*

Numbness May Be the Greatest Predator!

Look closely at what Paul said to a congregation he was shepherding:

> I wish you would bear with me while I indulge in a little [so-called] foolishness. Do bear with me!
>
> For I am zealous for you with a godly eagerness and a divine jealousy, for I have betrothed you to one Husband, to present you as a chaste virgin to Christ. But [now] I am fearful, lest that even as the serpent beguiled Eve by his cunning, so your minds may be corrupted and seduced from wholehearted and sincere and pure devotion to Christ.
>
> (2 Corinthians 11:1–3 AMP)

Paul wrote these words to Christians in Corinth. They weren't infidels or bad people—they were good people who, somewhere along the way, he knew could lose heart. The apostle feared they would succumb to the death of desire for God. Numbness may be the greatest predator threatening your Christian walk today!

As a spiritual father, the apostle was concerned about these people. He deeply loved them and was anxious over their journey. While I am no apostle Paul, I feel the same way about you and millions more who are at risk in the land of the spiritually shell-shocked and the emotionally dazed.

Paul shared his motive when he wrote, "[I care] because I have betrothed you to one Husband, to present you as a pure virgin to Christ." Then this great apostle said, "But I am afraid. I am fearful for you." The renowned Bible teacher Beth Moore, expressed the clearest interpretation of Paul's urgency. She said that the term for "fearful" might be better translated as: "I'm *terrified* for you, lest the evil one deceive you by his craftiness, that somehow he would deceive you and you would lose that pure, undefiled faith in Christ."

Do you remember what it was like when you first came to Christ, when you *knew* you were different because you had been washed by the blood of Jesus? Do you remember the joy you sensed when the lightbulb came on in your soul and you knew you had connected with the living God? It was good people like you Paul was talking to when he said, "I am *terrified* for you!"

Paul knew that evil, in some subtle way, may begin to strip us of our joy. He worried that in some way the con man and scam artist we call Satan would intercept us in the journey of life and steal away our pure, undefiled faith in Christ. God urges us in Proverbs 4:23, "Above all else, guard your heart, / for it is the wellspring of life" (NIV). But sometimes, pain leads us down a path where we actually are in danger of losing our hearts.

The truth is that if you are at a place of deep pain, then Paul the apostle and anyone else who really cares is "terrified for you." Are you broken or struggling in his journey because life is not the way it's supposed to be? Understand the cause and prepare to discover God's incredible solution to the problem. This is the place where everything you've been taught, or everything you have preached, over the years must come into play. You have to ask yourself, *Do I really believe it? Or is it all just myth?*

You're in a War

As Christians, we claim that "our citizenship is in heaven," and that is correct (Phil. 3:20 NIV). The downside to this is that kingdom of God is more than mere talk. The idea is that our conduct should reflect our citizenship.

If we have really been born from above, and if our lives have truly been "bought with a price"—the precious blood of Christ—then we should be different now (1 Cor. 6:20 NIV). If our behavior should reflect our citizenship, then let me tell you what you already know: there's a struggle going on!

The apostle Paul was sincerely terrified for good people he loved—he saw they were at risk. How do good people lose heart with God and life? By enduring enormous, unexpected, relentless pain.

I can still remember going to Bible camp as a young Pennsylvania boy. One of the very first verses we had to learn was James 1:2: "Brethren, count it all joy when you fall into various trials. . . ." I still dislike that passage because it talks about pain and suffering.

✦ *I hate pain. Suffering has no place on my wish list.*

To be frank, I get ill when I hear some untested and unscarred teacher stand up and quote that passage. It must be quoted because it is God's Word and it is true, but let it be quoted in tears and genuine humility before God and by people who have faced real risk in this life.

I hate pain. Suffering has no place on my wish list. Yet I know it will come nonetheless. According to the apostle Paul, even our planet itself gets in the act: "The whole creation has been groaning" for the day of redemption (Rom. 8:22 NIV).

Who wants darkness of soul or confusing days of struggle to be a part of his or her life? When enduring pain, most of us want to protest, "But this isn't the way it's supposed to be!"

My dad is a strong man who has battled cancer with God's help. Yet even after overcoming such hardship, he experienced one of those days.

Throughout his struggle with illness, he had looked forward to going back to the pulpit. He miraculously recovered and prepared for the day he'd anticipated for so long. Preaching was what he loved, what he held on to, especially since his wife of fifty years had passed away. But just two weeks before he was scheduled to return to his church, he got the word: "We don't want you back anymore."

The ambush caught him by surprise. *I don't understand. This isn't the way it's supposed to be.*

At the heart of our pain in times like these is the loss of control. We finally realize there is absolutely nothing we can do.

False expectations fuel disappointment in life. When people fail to hear the truth right up front, they believe that once they receive Christ, life will be completely pain free. God will take care of everything and meet all their needs—all they have to do is show up at church regularly. You and I know hardship befalls everyone.

What's Headed Your Way

Several years ago, Dr. Larry Crabb, a friend and mentor, shared with me, "Tim, you're a good man, but I feel you have an undernourished soul primarily because you haven't had much suffering." Then suddenly, devastating times hit—the circumstances of life ambushed me at the pass, and I faced the potential for loss of heart!

✦ *You have an undernourished soul primarily because
you haven't had much suffering.*

No, Larry didn't curse me, he blessed me. How many of us get such a clear warning from such a trusted and loving source about an impending ambush? To be forewarned is to be forearmed.

Jesus Himself warned us: "In this world you will have many trials and sorrows" (John 16:33 NLT). You know this. You know that persecution and tribulations come wrapped in all kinds of packages: loss, health problems, financial upsets, physical problems.

What happens during this ambush and assault stage is the making of us. It deeply impacts how we do life—and especially how we do relationship and intimacy with God and those we love. The enemy of your soul loves to be the silent donor to your misery. He fervently hopes for your demise.

Some armchair critics urge me to lay aside all of this talk about suffering and "just talk about getting beyond the past." I understand that, but a flood of pop psychologists and feel-good preachers will give you that information every day.

It is not enough. I want to help people win in *real life*. Temporary mental bandages and emotional pick-me-ups aren't enough—I want to show the Bible way to overcome the pain and sorrows we face.

✦ *Temporary mental bandages and emotional pick-me-ups
aren't enough!*

Long-Held Pain

I've closely examined the way Joseph, in the Old Testament, handled suffering. Many years after his brothers' brutal betrayal, he finally met up with them again in Egypt. The Bible tells us the pain Joseph released in that moment was so overwhelming and explosive that the entire house of the Egyptians heard his cries (Gen. 45:2).

After all those years had passed, and after achieving such prestige, power, and wealth—Joseph ranked second only to Pharaoh in one of the most powerful empires on earth—his brothers' rejection still hurt him deep inside. Why? Because that is the nature of pain.

What deep pain are you carrying? Do you want to learn how to succeed when the road gets long, overwhelming, and discouraging? Do you want to overcome what is now overcoming you? You can survive and overcome even when you begin to lose heart and question your call. God's power and undying love for you are at work even while you question who God is in your life!

Everybody will go through periods of disaffection or brokenness. But that is not what makes you as a man or woman. What makes you is *what you do with what's been dished out to you.* The sad truth is that most suffering has to do with our being flooded by things that just aren't right. Do you feel alone and in despair? I think God literally weeps with us during our broken times and declares to the cosmos, "It's enough." Have you ever sensed that?

> ✦ *What makes you is what you do with*
> *what's been dished out to you.*

But God is *for* you. The truth is that the evil one will hate you no matter what you do, but he will also *fear* you if you have surrendered your life to God. For that reason, it is no surprise that you are experiencing hellish assault.

✦ *Satan will fear you if you have surrendered*
your life to God.

Jesus warned about the dangers of love lost. He said, "And because lawlessness will abound, the love of many will grow cold. But he who endures to the end shall be saved" (Matt. 24:12–13). Why? Because the days are evil.

When life hammers you, you end up feeling empty and exhausted. Yet, because you were made for a heart full of hope and expectation, you cry out to God. You're hurt. You were expecting *something else*.

Just understand that when you get assaulted and ambushed in life, it naturally leads to what psychologists and counselors call "a double-A response." Your body kicks into a flight-or-flight response when you are frightened or threatened. When you get ambushed or assaulted, you get *angry* and/or *anxious*.

It is natural to respond to an ambush with anger or anxiety. It is supernatural to go beyond the response and grow even stronger in the process. Unfortunately, the path usually spirals downward from one double-A response to the next. In most cases, the next destinations on this descent into pain are the homes of anger and anxiety. We'll look at those emotions in the next two chapters.

Questions for Discussion and Reflection

1. Describe one or two dreams that remain unfulfilled or broken in your life.
2. Describe two current stressors that are tearing at your heart. Which is the most severe?
3. Draw a simple circle in your mind's eye and put yourself and your spouse in the middle of it. Now describe what stresses you have been up against. What competes for your affection for each other?
4. What is competing for your spiritual affection? What has been stealing that joy?
5. Consider whether the source of your stresses is one of these:

   * Circumstances and people beyond your control.
   * Your enemies—those who hate you.
   * Your own sins and failures.
   * The devil, to defeat and kill you.
   * Or God, to refine you by fire and cause spiritual growth in your life.

   What are the consequences in your thoughts, feelings, and behavior?
6. Has stress and suffering led you to draw closer to God or to pull away from Him? Do you feel confused about who God is and how He feels about you?
7. Has fighting the stressors of modern living leeched away your love of others? Has it drained away your compassion and care for those you normally love and care for?

Action Point: If you have been ambushed by life and are in deep pain, don't stop calling out to God and asking for His help. Today, tell Him all that you feel—including the disappointment and/or anger, hurt, despair. Ask for His aid in understanding and coping with your distress. Then listen for His answers. Stop the downward spiral right here.

· 2 ·

ANGER: THE FIERY FURNACE
OF THE SOUL
A Power for Good or Evil

The smoke hardly clears from the ambush site on your life before the forces of *anger* swarm upon the scene. Flesh and blood naturally respond to pain, perceived danger, injury, or attack.

We used to have a crazy dog named Bear that exhibited bizarre behavior when it was chow time. When old Bear started eating, he always wagged his tail like a somewhat normal, happy dog. But something about the movement of his wagging tail or his shadow made him go crazy. Bear would start foaming at the mouth, growling, hissing, and barking in a ferocious attack on his own tail. Perhaps he thought someone or something was trying to get his food. Regardless of the reason, this was crazy-dog behavior.

When someone feels violated or threatened in some way, the fight-or-flight response is instant and instinctive. When life isn't the way it is supposed to be—whether real or perceived—our natural response is to get angry: Angry at life. Angry at God. Angry at people. Angry at circumstances. And anger always finds an expression.

At this stage, the journey to loss of heart looks like this:

Losing Heart: The Descent into Pain
Ambushed and Assaulted
Anger

Are you filled with anger right now because life isn't the way it should be? Anger usually requires a trigger, a cause, even if we don't understand what it is at first. Triggers include but go far beyond the categories of betrayal, disappointment, accusation, and abuse.

Portraits of Anger

When I think of anger, my mind goes to a little guy with whom I was doing play therapy. As he colored a picture of his family, I was amazed at the fury that pored out of him. I thought he was going to drive the crayons through the paper as he shouted, "I'm a screw-up! I will never have any friends!"

I also think of an e-mail a friend sent not long ago that said, "Boy did we have it out last night. Tim, I got so mad at her, I picked up the new vase we were given as a wedding present and threw it across the room. It broke into a million pieces. She just makes me so mad!"

Bobby Knight, the celebrated basketball coach at Indiana University, also comes to mind. In 1995, during a game at Purdue University, he became so angry over what he considered an unfair call that he picked up a chair and threw it across the basketball court! Referees, players, and thousands of fans and television viewers around the world watched the drama explode before their eyes.

When thinking about anger, many people remember the Edmond Post Office Massacre in 1986, when an angry postal worker named Patrick Henry Sherrill killed fourteen coworkers and wounded seven before killing himself.

Investigators learned that Sherrill had a history of employment problems seemingly related to poor social skills. Apparently he launched his attack after receiving a negative review from supervisors. Anger was at the heart of the tragedy, an incident that is still considered one of the worst mass murders by a single gunman in U.S. history.

The sheer range of anger is astounding: it includes everything from feelings of mild irritation to waves of uncontrolled rage. Its impact is virtually universal because it affects the lives of the young and of the elderly—and everyone in between!

I sat next to an elderly man on a long flight, and as we talked I found him very likeable. A dad and his son sat in the seat directly in front of us, and the boy reminded me of my own son at that time (he had a little *energy*). I barely noticed, but evidently the elderly man paid close attention throughout the flight as the boy bounced around in his seat.

After we landed, everyone was gathering belongings when this elderly man reached forward, turned the boy around by the shoulders, and started yelling! He shouted at the child for being fidgety, and the boy was petrified!

Tears quickly formed in the boy's eyes as he asked his dad, "Dad, what's wrong with that man?" The dad turned to the elderly man and said, "You're crazy! What's up with you?"

Everyone was shocked, including me. Something triggered an explosive anger in this seemingly kind elderly man! He was huffing and puffing, and he became angry at everybody—

including me! His irrational anger made him oblivious to the feelings of that little boy.

Anger can endure for a brief nanosecond or stretch out over decades. We all get angry. In fact, some studies show that most of us get angry between eight and ten times a day.[1]

✦ *Most of us get angry between eight and ten times a day.*

This incident illustrates how the God-given emotion of anger can become the most destructive form of emotional cancer in a human being—what the Bible calls the "root of bitterness" (Heb. 12:15).

We Choose How to Handle Our Anger

Anger is an automatic emotion, but the *behavior* of anger—how we act on this emotion—is a choice. According to Gary and Carrie Oliver, experts on the subject of anger:

> Most people have no idea that anger is a secondary emotion that is usually experienced in response to a primary emotion such as hurt and fear. Anger can be an almost automatic response to any kind of pain.
>
> Anger is usually the first emotion we see. For males it's often the only emotion that they are aware of.[2]

> Anger is to our lives like a smoke detector is to a house, like a dash warning light is to a car, and like a flashing yellow light is to a driver. Each of those serve as a kind of warning or alarm to stop, look, and listen. They say, "Take caution, something might be wrong."[3]

In most cases, you become the first target of your anger. Sometimes you want to kick yourself and say, *How could I be so stupid? I should have known.* As Dr. Dan Allender puts it, "The initial cry of betrayal is 'What's wrong with *me?*' "[4]

Anger usually moves quickly to more satisfying targets, such as our peers or those under us in some way (including children, younger siblings, or coworkers). In the words of Dr. Allender, "We want someone to pay!"

> No one remains in his own self-contempt. Efforts to unearth an explanation for betrayal usually snap back to an equally harsh extreme: blaming the other. We magnify the betrayer's faults, list and recite his calumny.
>
> . . . Are we ever to be blamed for someone's sin against us? Absolutely not. . . . When sinned against, however, my response will typically be a sinful one: When I'm betrayed, I eventually betray others.
>
> . . . We want relief from our pain. We want someone to care and comfort us, but we also want justice, vengeance. The dark desire to make our betrayer pay places us in the strange position of being both a victim and an abuser.[5]

On the other hand, one of the God-ordained functions of anger is to motivate us to change the way things are. Anger, for instance, has inspired many of history's heroes to stand up against injustice, as their instincts of self-preservation warned them of danger.

Perhaps that is why Paul the apostle wrote such practical and down-to-earth words in Ephesians 4:26: "Be ye angry, and sin not: let not the sun go down on upon your wrath" (KJV).

Feeling Completely Bent Out of Shape

In the book *Sparkling Gems from the Greek*, author and missionary Rick Renner painted a vivid portrait of the Greek word translated as "anger" in this passage:

> The word "wrath" is the Greek word *paraorgismos*, a compound of the words *para* and *orgidzo*. The word *para* means *alongside*, as something that is *very close* to you. The word *orgidzo* is the Greek word for *wrath*, which depicts someone whose mood is so upset that he becomes completely bent out of shape over some issue.
>
> When *orgidzo* ("wrath") is operating in an individual, it often starts as silent resentment. That resentment slowly builds up inside the person, becoming stronger and stronger until one day, it finally explodes in rage! And because the resentment has simmered silently for so long, the outburst of explosive wrath is usually way out of proportion to the situation that caused the anger in the first place.
>
> But when these two words are joined together, forming the word *paraorgismos*, it presents the image of a person who brings anger to his side and then embraces it. Instead of rejecting anger or pushing it away when it shows up, this person draws it to himself and then nurses it, nourishes it, feeds it, and holds it close. The aggravating issue gets "under his skin" and soon becomes so entrenched that it becomes his constant companion and partner. He takes the offense with him wherever he goes—and that includes taking it to bed with him![6]

Anger is not the problem as much as *what you do* in your anger is. Anger is a God-given emotion, a state of preparedness to respond to a real or perceived wrongdoing or injustice in your life.

It is normal to get angry when you feel loss or when your

life is threatened in some way. The force of anger may literally save your life in these situations! But anger misdirected or nurtured into bitterness or rage is a very deadly bed partner.

✦ *Anger is not the problem as much as*
what you do *in your anger is.*

Perhaps this is why Paul warned us not to let the sun go down on our anger in Ephesians 4:26. He actually said that when we allow anger to last longer than a day and a night, we give the devil an "opportunity" (v. 27 NASB).

Anger most often seems to surface in my life when I feel betrayed. Perhaps you have managed to escape pain in your journey, but I have experienced painful situations when I felt friends had betrayed me or my close family members. I wanted to shake my fist at life (and a few of the individuals involved in the drama)!

Anger Everywhere

Did you know that the emotion of anger is something God Himself feels? The Bible is filled with references to the anger of God toward sin, toward rebellious people, and toward people who oppressed those who were loyal to Him.

In contrast to our mental pictures of angry people committing horrendous acts in fits of rage, Dr. Neil Clark Warren maintained we should have another picture featuring the anger of God:

The picture we need to have in our head is of the Lord God Almighty sending His own Son to earth . . . out of His anger.

You see, anger can be turned into the greatest expressions of love. For this reason, we have to become very clear about our definitions of anger, and aggression, of hate and hostility, and of how anger can be used in the service of your highest goals.

[In contrast,] that kick to the lawnmower, or obviously that hit to the side of your child's head—any aggressive act that is designed to bring harm to somebody or something—is a way of using your anger that is called "aggression."[7]

✦ *A tsunami of anger is overtaking the American culture.*

Road rage, church rage, shopper rage, sports rage, marital rage, and the American slang for work rage—"going postal": it seems everybody is ready to explode with anger over something! A tsunami of anger is overtaking the American culture. It wouldn't be so bad if the anger were channeled to produce positive change in our lives and culture, but sometimes it takes destructive forms. Some of the most common causes of anger include:

- ✦ Learned behavior (see Proverbs 22:24)
- ✦ Betrayal (see Proverbs 16:28)
- ✦ Feeling wronged (see Genesis 16:4–6, where both Sarah and Hagar felt wronged)
- ✦ Being put down (see Proverbs 15:1)
- ✦ Unmet needs (see Acts 6:1, where the Greek Jewish widows felt neglected)
- ✦ Stress and pressure of grief (see John 11:17–32, where Martha and Mary confronted Jesus when their brother, Lazarus, died)
- ✦ Disrespect (see Ephesians 5:24–6:4 concerning disrespect shown between spouses, children toward parents, and vice versa)

* Physical issues (including chronic pain and illnesses, severe medical treatments, high caffeine levels, etc.)
* Rebellion (see 1 Samuel 15:23, where rebellion is compared to the sin of witchcraft)

---

* *Children who live in a home-based cage of anger grow up to reproduce the same environment in their adult lives.*

Many people live in what I call *a cage of anger* in the confines of their own homes! Anger in America's marriages is exploding off the chart. The same thing goes for anger in the workplace. We know that children who live in a home-based cage of anger grow up to reproduce the same environment in their adult lives. After the deadly incident at the Edmond Post Office, corporations began to hire psychologists and behavioral experts to lower the stress factors in their work environments, and for good reason.

I've even seen the cage of anger surface in church congregations! Society's trend toward elevated anger levels is showing up more and more in churches across the nation. These congregations may be following unhealthy patterns set by their shepherds, or the sheep themselves may import unacceptable levels of anger to church life from worldly mind-sets and values.

These congregations tend to be strong on judgment but weak on mercy and grace — and that unbalanced mix shows up in the congregation's dealings with laymen or with its own leaders. Generally, you will see condemnation in abundance but evidence of a desire for reconciliation and restoration may be in very short supply.

Anger Will Always Find an Expression

We've learned a great deal about anger through God's Word and through accumulated human experience. One of the most important things we've learned is that anger will always find an expression—either negative (explosive) or positive!

We've also learned this: anger is an emotion skilled in the art of disguise.

Gary Oliver says that of all the emotions, anger is the one most likely to be mislabeled. Drs. Oliver and H. Norman Wright have outlined some of the most common disguises anger assumes in human behavior. (If you are breathing, you will probably find yourself somewhere on this list.)

> When we begrudge, scorn, insult, and disdain others or when we are annoyed, offended, bitter, fed up, repulsed, irritated, infuriated, incensed, mad, sarcastic, uptight, cross or when we experience frustration, indignation, exasperation, fury, wrath or rage, we are probably experiencing some form of anger. Anger can also manifest itself as criticism, silence, intimidation, hypochondria, numerous petty complaints, depression, gossip, sarcasm, blame, passive-aggressive behaviors such as stubbornness, half-hearted efforts, forgetfulness, and laziness.[8]

Again, though, Neil Clark Warren reminds us that "anger is a God-given capacity—a natural force which offers magnificent possibilities."[9] Our task is to recognize anger, understand its role in life, and learn how to release it in positive, productive ways.

Suppress It or Express It—It's Still Anger

Most of us handle anger in one of two ways: we *suppress* it or *express* it. Gary and Carrie Oliver expand on this idea by listing four "anger styles."[10]

1. Cream-Puffs: Repressed

These folks are passive, guilt-prone, and focused on protecting themselves and others to the point of remaining totally silent when hurt or abused. They will stuff down and hide any feelings of anger. Once the anger goes deep inside, they forget it is there and it becomes *repressed*. Cream-Puffs' anger is *implosive*. They may unknowingly express the anger in ways that hurt themselves and others. Anger, when finally handled God's way, can help motivate and move Cream-Puffs out of their dreary pain toward healthier and more constructive expression.

2. Locomotives: Explosive

Locomotives are always ready to blow off their heads of steam—even if it hurts everyone around them. They are often the reason Cream-Puffs go underground emotionally. Locomotives are aggressive reactors who tend to be insensitive to the needs and feelings of others. The anger of Locomotives is *explosive*, and they often communicate it in ways that violate the dignity and rights of others. This destructive style of anger, when given free rein, violates some of the most basic principles of the Christlike life.

3. Steel Magnolias: Passive-Aggressive

This metallic "flower" looks soft and tender on the outside, but if you attempt to cross this kind of person you'll discover a hard shell underneath. The problem is that Steel Magnolias almost exemplify the biblical "double-minded" people who are "unstable in all [their] ways" (James 1:8 NASB). In fact, the Greek term for "double-minded" in this verse means "two-spirited, vacillating in opinion or purpose."[11] You never quite know what these people will do—they appear calm on the outside but may be boiling cauldrons of bitter resentment on the inside. Sarcasm is one of their most effective tools against you or anyone else who crosses their paths. Anger is frequently at the core of passive-aggression, and no one can hide it entirely.

4. The Mature and Assertive Responder

This is the healthy option among the four. While the previous styles are dysfunctional, Mature and Assertive Responders make the most of God's gift of anger. There *is* a way to react to hurt or pain that allows us to "be angry and sin not," or God would have never commanded us to do it. These people act to repair or correct in what many call "righteous indignation." Perhaps the best way to understand the Mature and Assertive response is to see it contrasted point by point with its opposite—rage and resentment.

Richard Walters draws a clear comparison between the Mature and Assertive Responder's indignation and the resentment and rage we see in other anger styles.

> Rage seeks to do wrong, resentment seeks to hide wrong, indignation seeks to correct wrongs. Rage and resentment seek to destroy people, indignation seeks to destroy evil. Rage and resentment seek vengeance, indignation seeks justice. Rage is guided by selfishness, resentment is guided by cowardice, indignation is guided by mercy. Rage uses open warfare, resentment is a guerrilla fighter, indignation is an honest and fearless and forceful defender of truth. Rage defends itself, resentment defends the status quo, indignation defends the other person. Rage and resentment are forbidden by the Bible, indignation is required.

Rage blows up bridges people need to reach each other, and resentment sends people scurrying behind barriers to hide from each other and to hurt each other indirectly. Indignation is constructive: it seeks to heal hurts and to bring people together. Its purpose is to rebuild the bridges and pull down the barriers, yet it is like rage and resentment in that the feelings of anger remain.[12]

The Aggressive Response

Unfortunately, our most typical response to anger is aggression. We usually called aggressive people who are angry "hot-tempered" or "short-fused." But the Bible tells us:

+ An angry man stirreth up strife, and a furious man aboundeth in transgression. (Proverbs 29:22 KJV)
+ Do not associate with a man given to anger; / Or go with a hot-tempered man, / Or you will learn his ways / And find a snare for yourself. (Proverbs 22:24–25 NASB)

Perhaps you know people who express anger negatively. They have learned the power of their anger, and they often use it to control or dominate people. Have you ever been on the receiving end of one of these volcanic expressions?

It must have been the volcanic method of expressing anger Ben Franklin had in mind when he said, "Anger is seldom without reason, but seldom a good one."

You see the negative force of anger in the guy who comes home and slams his fist through the wall. Anger's negative power shows up in the little children who are so broken that all that pours out of them is rage! Their pain is so strong that you can't even talk to them.

Sometimes you see extremely angry parents shake their

children in vain attempts to get control. Exasperated and awash in anger, they often discipline their children too harshly. Discipline birthed out of anger only turns the focus off of the child's needs (i.e., parental emotional support and healthy discipline) and onto the parent's anger. Before long, the children start searching for the affirmation and validation they didn't receive from their parents. It is no wonder they go to drugs, alcohol, sexual promiscuity, and pornography.

A young person damaged by his parents' anger might express his hurt soul this way:

> Mom, Dad, this doesn't make sense to me. You're supposed to love me, Dad. You're not even around. Mom, you're hateful and mean to me. You don't even know me.
>
> Who are you? Who am I? How do I fit in? I'm fearful and anxious. I don't know what to do. I feel alone. You may think I'm cocky and arrogant, but the truth is I'm scared to death.
>
> And, yeah, I'm out there searching. But do you know why? It's because I don't know what to do or where to turn. I'm at a place right now where I can't seem to stop. I cry every night.

When people get confused, overwhelmed, or angry, they can become unstable. Essentially, they develop *divided hearts*.

The Divided Heart Is Unstable in All Its Ways

As we noted earlier, the meaning of the original Greek term translated as "double-minded" can be interpreted as being "two-spirited, vacillating in opinion or purpose," or having a divided heart. The divided heart is unstable in all its ways. It makes you uncertain about who to reach out to or where to go. The purpose of this book is to bring hope to good people who struggle on the journey of life, for whom anger may be a sticking point.

Difficulty and pain can create this divided heart, diverting us from the upward path and sending us on a descent into pain. This is where we discover we are losing heart. Our very souls feel divided in brokenness and hopelessness.

Proverbs 15:13 says, "By sorrow of the heart the spirit is broken." When I work with people experiencing loss, nearly every one of them wants to reach out to God. But they are just so angry that they strike out at anything and anyone who comes near them.

The people closest to them are most likely to be the safest (and therefore, the most likely) targets for their anger—this includes spouses, parents, children, and close friends. Until these people bring their anger under control, they continue using destructive patterns.

The Way Out

There is great hope for you—even when you feel helpless. Just as your life journey may lead you into disheartening circumstances, so the Lord God can lead you out.

King David experienced some of the deepest levels of emotional pain ever recorded in history. Yet he was the one who wrote under the inspiration of God: "The LORD is my shepherd; I shall not want. He maketh me to lie down in green pastures: he leadeth me beside the still waters. He restoreth my soul" (Ps. 23:1–3 KJV).

David was a real, flesh-and-blood man who felt pain and heartbreaking discouragement. He knew the red-hot flash of anger that could lead to murder. He knew the flush of bitter betrayal. Yet he also came to know the Shepherd who could lead him away from the battlefield and into green pastures of the soul, where he would find still waters and restoration.

Do you know someone who is filled with anger because life isn't the way it is supposed to be?

How about you? Are you fuming over something that has happened? Why? How long have you been frustrated inside? Can you see the path of anger in your own life?

What's sad is that when we don't make a course correction in our anger, life gets more complicated. For some, the downward spiral stops here, where they confront life's challenges and bring anger under control. For others—many others—the next dark step of descent is into deeper, more destructive anger.

Yet never forget that there is a way to come out of your pain and recover your heart!

Questions for Discussion and Reflection

1. Do you know someone who is filled with anger because life isn't the way it is supposed to be? How about you? Are you angry with someone or fuming over something that happened? Why? How long have you been frustrated inside? Can you see the path of anger in your own life?

2. Please recall the last time you were really angry at someone or about something. How did you express or suppress that anger? Have you ever witnessed someone else who has been in a fierce, out-of-control rage, throwing and destroying things? Describe it.

3. What is your primary style of anger expression? Are you more often a cream-puff, a locomotive, or a steel magnolia; or are you a mature and assertive responder?

4. Some define resentment as "anger with a history." Are there specific people you resent in your family? In your church? At your work? From your past?
5. Have you ever been physically sick, or do you have a chronic physical problem that you think may have been caused or influenced by your anger? Describe it.
6. Do you believe that God allows you to be angry, or were you raised to believe that all anger is wrong or sinful? Do you have any hope that your anger can be controlled and properly expressed?
7. Do you know anyone who expresses anger as God intends, and is a mature model of righteous anger? Describe what it would be like to be angry and yet not sin.

Action Point: If you are deeply angry, face it. Acknowledge the source and seek to remedy whatever ignited this often-destructive emotion. Do you know someone who handles anger well? Ask him or her to give you some guidelines. And don't forget to ask God to help you make a course correction today, so you'll keep from traveling further down the spiral.

· 3 ·

_____

ANXIOUS AND BARELY HOLDING ON
Life in the Shadow of Fear—
Just Beyond Hope

What do you do when your anger over injustice or assault doesn't solve anything? For a small dog beset by much larger dogs from the other side of the neighborhood, a loud bark and a sudden act of bravado sometimes do the trick. But what happens when the threat or fear just keeps coming?

When you still have that cornered feeling even as the white-hot heat of anger slowly drains from your tense body, something else takes its place. Shadows of fear begin to descend on your emotions, much as the shadows of day's end begin to lengthen over a land being covered by nightfall.

You may begin to feel that cold lump of uneasiness begin to form in your gut. It is normal to become fearful when what you expected seems dramatically and painfully different from what actually happens.

When someone sucker punches you, the next time that person comes around, you naturally display a hesitancy to come close again. You almost subconsciously reposition yourself for maximum protection because you aren't willing to become vulnerable again. Your journey looks like this:

Losing Heart: The Descent into Pain
Ambushed and Assaulted
Anger
Anxiety

When life isn't the way it is supposed to be and you can't resolve your plight no matter how hard you try, a fear response begins to take hold. You start looking for the next shoe to drop.

✦ *You start looking for the next shoe to drop.*

We must understand that fear is a normal emotion, just as anger is. We will feel fear when we are threatened.

Fear Can Be Good or Bad

A good dose of fear at the right time can save your life! Without it, you might be too slow to jump out of the way of a truck careening toward you on a city sidewalk. Faced with physical attack by an enemy or intruder, without fear you would be passive rather than instinctively combative or geared for survival.

Fear forces you to step back from the edge of a precipice where curiosity led you in the first place. Fear releases the explosion of adrenaline that helps you vault over the fence just three steps ahead of the angry bull—only later does your mind ask the obvious question, *How did I do that?*

Sometimes we experience more serious problems in life precisely because we refuse or fail to heed the warning fear gives us. At other times, we choose to fear the wrong things.

The teenager may fear social rejection more than the possibility of lifelong addiction to tobacco, alcohol, drugs, or a criminal lifestyle. The manager may fear losing his position more than losing his freedom and reputation when told to falsify the investment reports to the government. The pastor may fear appearing less than perfect before his flock more than he fears what may happen in his personal life three years later (when his health and faith begin to deteriorate from within).

This is the sad requiem of the life of King Saul in the Bible. When the prophet Samuel confronted Saul with his disobedience to God, Saul offered this sad excuse in an attempt to shift blame onto the people who put stress on him to follow their wishes: "I have transgressed the commandment of the LORD and your words, because I feared the people and obeyed their voice" (1 Sam. 15:24). (We'll look at this more closely in chapter 6.)

Signs of Fear's Residue

You may experience fear many times in your life, but God did not design you to live in a constant state of fear. Human beings forced to live in fear's toxic environment begin to exhibit telltale symptoms.

✦ *God did not design you to live in a constant state of fear.*

The signs inevitably show up in our behavior: the abused child who invariably ducks anytime an adult raises a hand, the abused spouse who winces or shrinks back when a voice is raised, the unhealed war veteran who finds himself dropping to the ground and shouting "Incoming!" when a car backfires, or the victim of childhood sexual abuse who suddenly finds she can't respond physically to the husband she loves.

These are the unwilling trophies of fear.

At the most toxic levels, fear seems to accelerate the human dying process physically while extending and worsening the pain mentally. It seems that fear is the mother of many of our psychological and physiological complaints and ailments.

Indeed, doctors say their patients complain about stress, anxiety, and other related emotional and physical symptoms more than anything else—regardless of whether they are seeking help for physical or psychological ailments.[1]

An estimated 20 million Americans experience nervous tension, sleep disturbances, physical aches and pains, and many other symptoms due to these conditions. In fact, stress, anxiety, and related depression are now considered epidemic and the leading mental health disorders in our nation.[2]

Anxiety compromised the thinking of even the wisest man in the world. We see fear's influence on Solomon in this verse from Ecclesiastes 9:11: "I returned, and saw under the sun, that the race is not to the swift, nor the battle to the strong, neither yet bread to the wise, nor yet riches to men of understanding, nor yet favor to men of skill; but time and chance happeneth to them all" (KJV).

When Anxiety Takes Over

Jesus said, "Do not be anxious about your life" (Matt. 6:25 ESV). Paul the apostle echoed the Lord's words when he said, "Be anxious for nothing, but in everything by prayer and supplication with thanksgiving let your requests be made known to God" (Phil. 4:6 NASB).

When anger fails to bring immediate relief from a perceived danger or source of pain, anxiety takes the wheel of your life. Where once you expected to find safe places in your life, anxiety becomes your new 24/7 companion.

When you live at 2407 Anxiety Court, you develop a broken place where you ask the first question of the wounded: *why?* This question echoes through your conscious and unconscious mind day and night. You pray, "God, why do You allow all this stuff to go on in my life? Why can't You solve it? I've prayed. I've begged You. I've done everything. Just look at all of those people over there. They live like hellions and their lives are easy. Now look at mine! Why?"

We rarely, if ever, receive the answers to that question. When nothing comes to soothe our pain, we begin to reach out for anything that appears to offer consolation. We are at great risk in that state of vulnerability.

When we leave the problem and process in God's hands, He sends us safe harbors of reassurance, encouragement, and help. I remember the times my wife, Julie, and I visited her grandma in her last days of life. She would reach out to take my hand, then ask, "Tim, when do you think God's going to take me home? I'd rather be at home."

✦ *When we leave the process in God's hands, He sends us safe harbors of reassurance, encouragement, and help.*

Grandma was secure about her final destination with the Lord, but she had control over very few things at that stage of her life. She just wanted someone to talk to. In her case, she had settled the big question of *who* and she didn't seem too anxious about *why*. She just needed reassurance about *when*.

Two experts explain that it's the not knowing that hurts the most:

> The problems we face, even the big ones, aren't so bad. It's the unexplained ones that scare us to death. We're not nearly so bothered by the size of a problem as we are by its degree of mystery. It's not knowing what's wrong that arouses the worst terror. Mystery scares us because it puts us out of control and leaves us with an option we don't naturally like—to trust someone besides ourselves.
>
> . . . Many people are struggling with problems they have not yet been able to adequately explain. It's as if they are permanently trapped in that moment of terror before the doctor looks up from the lab report to tell them what's wrong. They've asked, "What's wrong?" but no one has answered. And that's scary. Unexplained problems bother us the most.[3]

When you can't resolve the challenges of life with anger and anxiety takes over, again, you tend to get tentative about living. You become like the bird dog that has become gun-shy. You can no longer do what it is in your very nature to do. It becomes difficult or impossible to enjoy what you used to love.

One lady who had come to me for marriage counseling said, "I don't want to love him anymore. You don't understand—all he does every time I try is *hurt me*. He just stabs me [with his words and behavior]. Please don't let me go back there again. That's not the way it's supposed to be, is it? Surely God doesn't want me to be hurt over and over again by him!"

Even Healers Hurt

What happens when we find the very healers we hope will bring us relief are actually suffering from the same ailments that plague us?

John Ortberg, a highly respected pastor, psychologist, and mentor to thousands, shared the following during a lecture at the 2001 AACC World Conference: "Seems to me that you don't have to scratch very far underneath the surface in a whole lot of churches that a lot of us are involved in to find leaders who are as driven and unsettled and anxious and angry and envious and exhausted as anybody outside the church."[4]

Everyone must deal with the effects of anxiety in life—and that even includes pastors, psychologists, doctors, commercial airline pilots, schoolteachers, and law enforcement officers. We already know that "hurt people can hurt people," but people in the throes of anxiety can cause damage to others as well.

Even good parents enduring a bad day can inflict careless threats on their children. *Every* parent makes mistakes he or she regrets, and children who are loved well manage most of these mistakes well. Yet, parents and caregivers who listen to the inner voice of God can avoid causing even these "innocent" wounds.

✦ *Parents and caregivers who listen to the inner voice of God can avoid causing even these "innocent" wounds.*

John Ortberg bared his soul in his lecture before the counselors attending our American Association of Christian Counselors convention for one reason: he wanted to help them avoid the misstep God pointed out to him. In the process, he described one of those painful family visits to the mall with three preschool-age children with the goal of taking a happy family photo. John called it "a brutal experience." He said he went through several parental mental stages, beginning with "naive optimism." That one ended abruptly when the children saw the strange photo contraption and erupted in tears. As hopes grew dim for a usable Christmas picture, John moved into the bribery stage. He hinted at a trip to the sugary ice-cream-laden pie shop if all went well by some miracle, but that didn't last long either.

> Then I moved on to the third level—the threatening stage [this is the place to acknowledge that you, too, have sinned and fallen short of the parenting of God].
> "If you kids want to cry, I'll give you something to cry about!" It's a very effective way to motivate kids—I learned about that in developmental psychology a long time ago.
> So things just went from bad to worse, and by this time the lobby was filled with other people. . . .
> When our middle child just lost control over the situation, I finally pulled her aside and said, "Mallory, I bet that more than anything else in the world you wish you had Baby Tweezers" (her first doll and her favorite one).[5]

The parental misstep was only seconds away as John Ortberg continued his public confession about what may be called parent-inflicted family trauma: "She couldn't even trust herself to talk. There were big tears in her eyes, and her lower lip was sticking out so far a bird could perch on it. That was when I said to her, "Well, Mallory . . . *if you ever want to see Baby Tweezers alive again . . .*"

> I'm not proud of it. . . . [I did it] because I wasn't concerned about what was happening inside my children's spirit. I

didn't stop and think about the fear or confusion or anything else they'd be feeling. I was just in a hurry—and for no particular reason.

I had no meetings to attend, I had nothing on my list of things to do. I was just in a hurry.[6]

Is John Ortberg a bad dad? No, he is an exemplary father. This is a cautionary tale to help you and me avoid hurting the people we love every day. It may also help you heal from wounds you may be carrying around this moment!

I wish all of our childhood wounds were this mild and curable, just as I wish all parents were as loving, caring, and transparent as Dr. Ortberg, but life is often much more difficult. In fact, by the time you find yourself suffering from anxiety, you may perpetually be telling anyone who will listen, "Life just isn't supposed to be this way!"

What Part Stress Plays

If fear is the basic emotion behind anxiety, then anxiety is fear on steroids. Stress is another contributor to the anxiety mix. Stress may be described *as the effects of outward and inward pressure on your physical body.*

✦ *Anxiety is fear on steroids.*

Most of the emotional or behavioral symptoms of stress in your life will occur within three months after the ambush—you lose your job, go through a divorce, survive the car wreck, or get the promotion (to more responsibility and tougher deadlines) you wish you had never accepted. The sources of stress in your life may come from almost any area in your life, but most of them come and go and you negotiate the rapids without lasting problems.

Three months later, other symptoms of stress may show up in your body or behavior. If these symptoms last less than six months, clinicians might say you are suffering from *acute stress.* If they go on for longer than half a year, you might be diagnosed with *chronic stress.* This is the kind of stress that, if not dealt with, could weaken your immune system and possibly damage your health and well-being.[7]

As bad as stress sounds, anxiety is even worse.

Anxiety can be caused by stress, and it can *add* to your stress. One dictionary says the English word "anxious" comes from the Latin word *anxius.* What caught my eye is the next phrase in the word history—the editor noted that *anxius* "is akin to *angere*—to strangle, distress"![8]

That is exactly what anxiety tries to do to your body, your soul, and your mind! Should we be surprised that so many people suffering from anxiety show up in emergency rooms presenting physical complaints of severe breathing problems? The dictionary reference actually refers the reader to further investigation with another amazing phrase: "More at *Anger*"!

The long list of descriptions offered for *anxious* and *anxiety* included: "extreme uneasiness of mind or brooding fear about some contingency, painful or apprehensive uneasiness of mind usually over an impending or anticipated ill, an abnormal and overwhelming sense of apprehension and fear often marked by physiological signs (as sweating, tension, and increased pulse), by doubt concerning the reality and nature of the threat, and by self-doubt about one's capacity to cope with it."[9]

The Way Your Body Reacts

Basically, your body responds the same whether it is dealing with fear, stress, or anxiety. It begins with the initial fear response we've discussed already. Stress or anxiety just make the response last longer, and it doesn't matter to your body whether your problem is physical danger or something you've imagined!

When you get down to it, one of the key differences between your responses to fear and danger, stress, or anxiety is duration—the length of time it takes before you show signs of recovery.

In some cases, it is virtually impossible for us to recover without help. Some might feel this is a statement of doubt, but I'm convinced it is a statement of reality endorsed by God's Word and provided for by His provision through the Christian community and the wisdom of God in the Scriptures.

God commands us to restore those overtaken by sin and bear one another's burdens (Gal. 6:1–2), to rejoice with those who rejoice and weep with those who weep (Rom. 12:15), to forgive if we hope to be forgiven ourselves (Matt. 6:12, 14), and to confess our sins one to another and pray for each other (James 5:16). Even when Isaiah alluded to Jesus the Messiah in Isaiah 50:4, he said, "The Lord GOD hath given me the tongue of the learned, that I should know how to speak a word in season to him that is weary." If that isn't counseling, then please tell me what it is!

When anger over a crisis changes into anxiety, watch for the recurrence of these symptoms over periods longer than three months:

+ Fast heart rate
+ Rapid or shallow breathing

+ Increased muscle tension
+ Loss of concentration
+ Diarrhea
+ Substance abuse
+ Avoidance behaviors
+ Disturbances in sleep or appetite patterns
+ Repetitive behaviors
+ Intrusive thoughts
+ Interpersonal conflict
+ Depression

When you talk with others about how you feel, are you using terms such as these?

+ tense
+ on edge
+ uptight
+ hassled
+ nervous
+ jittery
+ jumpy
+ wound up
+ scared
+ terrified
+ insecure
+ pressured
+ alarmed
+ anxious
+ worried
+ dreading what might happen
+ uncertain
+ vulnerable
+ apprehensive
+ edgy
+ troubled[10]

Many times we suffer long-term wounds psychologically just as we do physically. When the effects of anxiety show up and remain in your life consistently over a lengthy period of time, you may be the victim of trauma.

Another Piece of the Puzzle: Trauma

Trauma simply means "wound," but it is also used to describe "a disordered psychic or behavioral state resulting from mental or emotional stress or physical injury."[11]

A national epidemic swept across America during the terrorist attacks of 9/11. As millions felt alarm, thousands found their overstressed bodies and minds responding to that threat with classic symptoms of post-traumatic stress disorder.[12]

What is post-traumatic stress disorder (PTSD)? It was called "shell shock" in World War I, "combat fatigue" in World War II, and PTSD beginning in 1980. Perhaps the best definition of PTSD is *feeling as if you walk around in a state of shock.*

Do you experience a traumatic event in your life over and over again in your memories, dreams, or waking flashbacks? None of these things are necessarily bad in and of themselves, but when they retrigger that anger-or-anxiety response in your body or cause you to avoid "thoughts, feelings, people, places, situations, or conversations connected to the trauma," they can begin to do real damage.[13]

You may begin to feel very nervous, even when you have no apparent reason for it. You may find it difficult to sleep, concentrate, and you live on pins and needles. At this point you may be suffering from exaggerated anxiety and living in a body flooded with increased adrenaline and sympathetic nervous system activity. That can cause short-term and long-term disruptions in organs and body systems![14]

One of the amazing elements of PTSD is that people don't *remember* past events—they *relive* them over and over again. My heart goes out to people who find it hard to drive a car because of persistent memories of the serious accident that nearly killed them when they were young. I ache for the young rape survivors who feel they can't breathe every time memories of violent attacks resurface in their minds.

Perhaps you have met adults who remain deathly afraid of water because in childhood they were thrown into deep water and told to "sink or swim," or who simply fell off a dock or boat into deep water and nearly drowned.

The term *post-traumatic stress disorder* may sound terribly technical, but we have a large number of people in our families, churches, and communities struggling with this problem. If you are one of those wounded people—if you have tried to do everything you know to do, but you still suffer thoughts of doubt and constant crises of faith—then you know what I'm talking about.

You are not whole, you are *hurt*! You would love to live a normal life, but it seems to elude you no matter what you do. I encourage you to talk with your pastor, a good friend, a qualified Christian counselor—just find someone you can talk to who understands, who will give you Christ-centered care. Too many people wrestling alone with this extreme form of anxiety end up battling thoughts of suicide (20 percent) or developing extra problems as well, including depression and alcohol or drug abuse.[15] You do not have to become one of those statistics.

✦ *You would love to live a normal life, but*
it seems to elude you no matter what you do.

Rely on God's Love

Is it a sin to experience disaffection toward God because of anxiety in your life? Only if you cling to it. What should you do if you have thoughts of suicide? Tell someone about them. Seek help. Don't do what Saul did—don't fear what people may think. Remember that God loved and valued you so much that He sent His own Son to save you!

Don't try to deal with severe anxiety or PTSD alone. Talk to your pastor, a good friend, a qualified Christian counselor— someone who understands and can guide you with Christ-centered care.

When you suffer assaults or attacks in your life, you *will* respond with anger or anxiety. When anger doesn't work, anxiety takes over. In time, you may begin to question God and wonder if He really loves you.

Who experiences disaffection toward God? I'm convinced *every one of us* battles this sometime in our lives. The very reason I'm writing these words to you today is to help you go all the way through the process—whether your journey through the loss of heart is quick or long and difficult.

How are you doing? Is your heart filled with questions? Do you feel tentative? Do you feel fearful? Are you waiting for the next shoe to drop?

If you can't resolve your plight in your anger and anxiety, it leads to another difficult place—one that you were not made for. Unfortunately, there is a lot of company there.

Just keep this fact in mind—*there is a way through.* You *can* recover your heart and come out of your pain!

Questions for Discussion and Reflection

1. Describe the last time you were afraid. What was the context or situation? When you are afraid, what does your body tell you? What thoughts race through your mind?

2. What are your biggest fears? Have you ever thought about what you fear the most: Failure? Being seen as less than perfect? Losing a position? Losing a loved one? Abandonment? Fear of others hurting you?

3. What symptoms are you aware of that may point to an underlying fear in your life?

4. Are you suffering from traumatic fear or post-traumatic stress disorder? What are you doing to get help to resolve this?

5. Fear is ultimately the result of feeling unsafe in life and relationships. What makes you feel safe? What does it take to calm you down—what thoughts, self-talk, actions or other methods do you use?

6. How do you rely on God to manage or resolve your fears in living?

Action Point: If anxiety is controlling your life and affecting your health, put aside the "why" question, which is seldom answered. Instead, exert your energy in seeking ways to eliminate, subdue, or cope better with the source of anxiety. If you can't regain control by yourself, find competent professional help. You don't have to live this way any longer!

· 4 ·

_____

ALONE AND WOUNDED
IN AN UNCARING WORLD
Imitation Life on a
Very Small, Self-Made Island

It is only natural to withdraw from others to find some peace when life is not the way it is supposed to be. When you can't resolve your hurt and pain and you feel overwhelmed by your anger or anxiety, what do you do to regain some sense of control over your life?

How many of the people you know right now feel alone? Most of them probably faded into the background even while their hearts ached for something more. They may be alone by choice, but they hate the aloneness. They're on self-made desert islands, hiding from rescue planes.

We *all* go through periods when life doesn't seem fair, when all we want to do is run and hide. One woman revealed the deep pain of her heart when she asked, "What do you do when someone repeatedly knocks the wind out of you? After you've tried and tried to get him to listen, to stop hurting you? You just have to pull away. I just can't take the meanness and the lack of respect anymore."

In a way, this woman's decision to withdraw from the pain-giver seems to be a reasonable response to an unreasonable situation. But just after the creation of the first man, a voice far greater than that of any human declared, "It is not good that man should be alone" (Gen. 2:18 KJV).

God is *always* right.

As the descent toward loss of heart continues, aloneness becomes the constant companion you never asked for and seldom welcome.

Losing Heart: The Descent into Pain
Ambushed and Assaulted
Anger
Anxiety
Aloneness

The State of Aloneness

I will never forget the pain I heard in another woman's voice as she cried out to me over the phone: "Tim, the man who meant more to me than anybody in my whole life was my dad. He rescued me from abuse!"

Her mother had victimized her at the age of six. "My daddy fought for me, he got me out of all of it, loved me when no one else was there. Four years ago, when my marriage was going bad, my dad died. Do you know what it's like to feel all alone?"

When fear and anxiety run rampant through your life, you usually move further downward in your journey to the loss of heart. One day you discover you have moved into the state of aloneness. In this state, every resident feels as if he is alone and wounded in an uncaring world.

✦ *When fear and anxiety run rampant through your life, you usually move further downward in your journey to the loss of heart.*

John Donne knew something wasn't right about this way of thinking. This noted poet, philosopher, and clergyman wrote in 1624, "No man is an island, entire of itself; every man is a piece of the continent, a part of the main."[1] In essence, he was saying that we were made for relationships. We are broken in relationship and we are healed in relationship. When one person hurts, we all hurt. When one person gets better, we all get better. When one person gives up, we all lose something valuable.

The problem is that when you can't resolve the challenges in your life, anxiety overtakes and discourages you. Then you become more alone as you distance yourself from every possible source of pain.

The descent toward the loss of heart is gradual, and it seems to come in stages:

- ✦ When you feel angry, you go against people.
- ✦ When you feel anxious, you begin to move away from people.
- ✦ When you feel alone, you begin to withdraw completely.

People suffering from anger, anxiety, or long-term traumas become hypervigilant. When you feel unlovely, unworthy, and unaccepted for some reason, you may feel your only option for relief is to avoid every potential source of pain.

When life feels out of control and your emotions are all

over the map, you naturally want to run! You feel like the old cartoon character, Fred Flintstone, in his prehistoric foot-driven car. You can go one hundred miles an hour with those feet! You just want to run, run, run until you move away from the dangers and pain of engagement with God and man. You are desperate to reach the supposed safety zone away from everyone.

Trouble in the "Safety Zone"

The fact is that this phase of aloneness brings a whole new set of problems! In a way, we begin to act like wounded animals, pulling in every exposed portion of our bodies to protect ourselves from attack. The anger and anxiety triggered by assault remove all feelings of safety. They drive us to duck for cover. At that point, the only safe conclusion is that only *one* person has your best interest at heart—*you*! Very little talk goes on in this dark, hunkered-down bunker called Aloneness.

✦ *Anyone who goes too far alone goes mad.*

Aloneness is a dangerous place and a false hope. As the Jewish proverb warns us, "Anyone who goes too far alone goes mad." The book of Proverbs echoes this warning with divine authority: "A man who isolates himself seeks his own desire; / He rages against all wise judgments" (Prov. 18:1).

Just as African lions on the hunt work tirelessly to separate their prey from the rest of the herd, so will the toothless lion of hell work tirelessly to pry you away from other people and ultimately from God. The adversary knows that if he can get you *alone*, his chances of removing you from the picture rise significantly—and so do his opportunities to spread pain to countless others.

✦ *The adversary knows that if he can get you* alone, *his chances of removing you from the picture rise significantly.*

The woman who feels alone in her marriage cries out: "All I've ever wanted is for somebody to love me. He's not there for me. I don't feel safe. I don't feel significant anymore!" Very often, people direct such barrages of pain-filled blame toward God as well: "And where are *You*, God? You're not taking care of me either. I prayed for my husband, I prayed for my kids, I prayed for our finances, and I still feel alone. It feels as if You're not there for me."

"Yes, God Is Good, *But* . . ."

This has been the *modus operandi* for evil ever since the first seduction in the Garden of Eden. Consider what the serpent did with Eve. He was too cunning to challenge God's virtue directly, so he talked Eve into believing a single small lie: "Yes, God is good, but He has withheld one thing from you."

Your enemy doesn't have to have you in the gutter to claim a victory. All he needs is a little doubt to mix up and contaminate your view of God. He wants you to believe that while God is *mostly* good, there is also a part of Him that isn't necessary good toward *you*.

If you ask most people—even Christian people—who are in crisis, "Do you think God is good?" they may quickly complete the memorized mantra: "Oh yeah, He's good all the time.

God is good." But deep in their hearts, many of them silently add the phrase, *He's just not good to* me.

If you were to ask why they felt exempt from God's goodness, you might hear something like, "That's because . . . well, I don't know why. I don't know if it's me, or something I've done. I'm confused." They are not alone. Even the greatest of theologians have wrestled with this issue called "the problem of pain."

When you enter the state of aloneness, you find yourself full of confusion. It is easy to cut confused folks out of the herd of regular folks. That is why the enemy uses aloneness to separate you from your friends, and you begin to think: *They don't understand—I honestly don't believe they even care anymore.* He is especially eager to sever you from your Bible study, prayer partners, or cell group, making you think, *Nothing we do there really applies to my problem. They really don't understand or care about me anyway. And I'm not sure prayer works anymore.* He hopes to limit your appetite and access to God's Word and the nurturing support found in Christian fellowship.

Once he convinces you it is a painful waste of time to regularly attend church with other Christians, it is inevitable that you will stop thinking about "whatever is true, whatever is honorable, whatever is right, whatever is pure, whatever is lovely, whatever is of good repute" (Phil. 4:8 NASB).

Author Donald Miller accurately described some of the feelings of aloneness in his book *Blue Like Jazz*:

> I know about that feeling, that feeling of walking out into the darkness. When I lived alone it was very hard for me to be around people. I would leave parties early. I would leave church before worship was over so I didn't have to stand around and talk. The presence of people would agitate me. I was so used to being able to daydream and keep myself

company that other people were an intrusion. It was terribly unhealthy.[2]

✦ *Healing for your hurts is nowhere to be found*
in stinking thinking patterns!

When Lies Take Over

This is where the pattern of "stinking thinking" begins to set in.
Internal lies begin to intensify and supplant healthy thoughts
about life: *Life's not fair. God is unkind.* No matter how hard
and long you search for it, healing for your hurts is nowhere to
be found in stinking thinking patterns! (We'll talk more about
these in chapter 13.)

I've mentioned the old maxim: "Hurt people hurt people."
People who feel alone often become terribly aggressive. In their
desperation to avoid pain, they may actually run over other
people in the process! It's like someone so desperate to escape
a fire that he tramples the people in front of him in his blind,
headlong rush for safety.

Perhaps the saddest part of this picture is that even during
the times you feel most alone, your heart still cries out, "I just
wish *somebody* would love me." This is the true longing running
through your soul.

In church, surrounded by Christian people professing to
love their fellow man, you feel the tears pour down your face
unnoticed. While I hope most of the people around you would
be quick to help in your time of need, the truth is that there
are a million reasons they might not notice your pain, and asking another person for help is perhaps the last thing you want
to do when you feel alone.

Lonely People Avoid the Very Cure to Their Loneliness

It is very common for lonely people to avoid the very cure to their loneliness, self-defeating though it may seem. In fact, the avoidance of people—and on a larger scale, agoraphobia, the fear of open or public places—is often linked with anxiety.

Why is it such a problem to feel so alone? Everyone needs his or her "space," his or her private times away from others. Personal space isn't the aloneness we're talking about. This is the kind of aloneness no one really wants—it feels more like a prison cell than a place of refreshment. The feeling of aloneness birthed through anxiety or anger is painful because we simply weren't made to be alone, as I've noted.

It is more than ironic—it was intentional—that Jesus experienced the pain of anxiety just before He endured the most complete and destructive form of aloneness ever experienced by a man: death.

✦ *Our Savior cried out in terms that perfectly describe
the feelings of anyone who has felt truly alone.*

As He was dying on the cross, our Savior cried out in a loud voice from the depths of His soul in terms that perfectly describe the feelings of anyone who has ever felt truly alone: "My God, my God, why hast thou forsaken me?" (Matt. 27:46 KJV).

How many lonely people do you know? How many of your family members, friends, and acquaintances are going through brokenness right now? How many of them feel assaulted and abandoned by life, by God, and by other people?

Part of the problem is that so few of us have people we can

really talk to in times of trouble. Even our best friends fall short in the patience category. They grow too weary too soon; even before we can explain our pain, they rush to cheat us of the opportunity to honestly deal with our emotions. We're not even allowed to cry out as Jesus did and say, "God, why did You forsake me in this? It doesn't seem fair." It seems to me that Jesus, the Son of God, already knew the full plan. He knew why it had to be, but as a man He needed to express His emotions. So do we.

✦ *As a man He needed to express His emotions. So do we.*

Instead, our brave attempt to bare our souls in search of healing may be cut short with such one-sentence "cures" as "Shut up and quit your murmuring. Things could be worse!"

You may be thinking, *No, right now life isn't okay. It is not well with my soul! At this very moment in my garden of suffering, I also want the cup to pass from me! I want the same privilege my Savior had when He honestly expressed His emotions to His Father with the prayer, "If it be Your will, let this cup pass from Me, God."*

How Many Would Be Spared If We Listened?

Sometimes I wonder how many of us would be spared the descending sorrows of alienation if someone had only listened when we first felt alone. The truth is that the downward spiral toward disaffection with God can be stopped and the ascent to wholeness begun at any point.

Evil flourishes when you feel alone. The enemy begins to

wring his gnarled hands when he notices you are convinced that no one understands or really cares about your soul. And that is a dangerous place to be.

When you feel alone, you try to find anchor points anywhere on the slippery slope of your life. You feel yourself falling, and you know it's getting worse, not better. You keep trying to hang in there but you have nothing to hold on to.

In this hypervigilant state, you become more sensitive to minor upsets. You find yourself exploding in anger or frustration over nothing. At this stage of the journey, you experience the Ecclesiastes syndrome, where "all the labor of man is for his mouth, / And yet the soul is not satisfied" (Eccl. 6:7).

When we live with unsatisfied souls, we will pour almost anything into them to appease our hunger. Why? Again, it is because God made us for relationship and connectedness. And when something goes wrong despite everything we've tried to do, we are left with the lonely cry, *It's not supposed to be this way!*

The Wounds of Our Friends Can Scar Our Souls

Even people who love us can inspire isolation. If most of our pain comes from those closest to us, our solution is to pull away. One of the invariable facts about relationships is that when it comes to wounds of the soul inflicted by friends or family members, *the closer they are, the more damage they do.*

That is what tears deeply into our souls, the fabric of who we are. The wounds of our friends can scar our souls. Even if the wounds are accidental and inadvertent, they often leave us filled with discouragement and confusion.

It can cause the most gentle of souls to slam their fists against a wall! Through the anger, the anxiety, and in the very midst of our aloneness, we are really crying out in our spirits.

I think God understands that. After all, it was God who invented emotions and carefully linked them with our thoughts, our capacity for logic, and our spirits.

✦ *Some of the suffering we endure in life has nothing to do with any particular cause or effect.*

While some of our suffering in this life is directly linked to our sin (and ultimately to our fallen state as descendants of Adam), I'm convinced that some of the suffering we endure in life has nothing to do with any particular cause or effect. We simply live in a dark world that is groaning and travailing for its own day of redemption.

We live in a physical environment where things fall due to the law of gravity, and they sometimes hurt us. Bacteria, viruses, and other microorganisms constantly test our God-given protection barriers.

Even without the external factors, our bodies sometimes don't work properly. We may suffer from chemical imbalances, organ malfunction, autoimmune reactions to our own bodies, or just the pain of worn-out parts.

Above all, we live with sinful people who are going to hurt us from time to time. Even the best Christians can be inconsiderate at times and not know it.

And so we respond. Without even becoming aware of it, we unintentionally sever our emotional ties to those who could most easily mend our thoughts and feelings of being alone.

For instance, I've found that brokenness in marriage relationships is usually rooted in the unintentional severing of emotional ties. So much is working against our affection for each other that it can boggle the mind. We contribute to it ourselves through our own sin and selfishness.

Spouses and parents, for instance, devote so much time and energy rushing from place to place that they don't devote time and effort to creating and preserving meaningful relationships with each other and their children.

✦ *The more you love, the deeper the sorrow in your heart.*
That is because love is painful.

Wasted Time

Much of our sorrow seems to be tied to missed opportunities. When we feel we've "missed it" for some reason, we live with regret. Many people find themselves saying, "I wish I had spent more time with my dad." Others gaze wistfully at photos of their grown children who never visit and say, "I should have spent more time with my children when they were little. Now my career is over and my children won't have anything to do with me."

People who love much, grieve much. I firmly believe that the more you love, the deeper the sorrow in your heart when you lose your loved ones, or experience a broken or severed relationship. That is because love is painful.

It is only natural that your spirit cries out for something else. God made you for wholeness.

We see the final portrait in John's vision of our heavenly experience, where he says, "And God shall wipe away all tears from their eyes; and there shall be no more death, neither sorrow, nor crying, neither shall there be any more pain" (Rev. 21:4 KJV).

Isaiah the prophet saw our destiny from afar: "The crooked shall be made straight, and the rough places plain. . . . He shall feed his flock like a shepherd: he shall gather the lambs with his arm, and carry them in his bosom, and shall gently lead those that are with young" (Isa. 40:4, 11 KJV).

Perhaps I'm growing more sentimental, but once I reached middle age, reality peeled back those youthful years and I could see how much time I've wasted. I understood how many relationships slipped by because I didn't expend any effort to maximize them. It made me want to live every moment from then on.

More and more people are getting stuck in this place of extreme loneliness today. Perhaps we have lost something from the good old days.

In the Good Old Days

In the times before we learned to live at the speed of light, before we scattered across the nation and the world to make our livings, Grandma and Grandpa, perhaps with Great-Grandfather and Great-Grandmother, lived within a few miles of Mom and Dad and all of the aunts and uncles.

Many families used to witness life and death in close proximity to one another. Whatever they did, they did it together. A genuine sense of community seemed to bind lives together and provide a security that we sorely miss today.

Disconnected societies produce disconnected and lonely people. It could be argued that we're closer together today than we've ever been due to technology. But despite our growing skills at pushing buttons and communicating through modern media, we are more isolated and alone than we've ever been.

✦ *Disconnected societies produce disconnected
and lonely people.*

Busy, hurried lives lead to gnawing fatigue. We may have our lives wrapped around computers, but we are not computers ourselves! We get tired. Fatigue leads to irritability—which directly affects every relationship in our lives.

Irritability leads to isolation. When you come home tired, the next thing you know you are yelling, "Shut up! Straighten up this house." And all those within earshot say, "You big grouch!" and move away to the nearest "safe" room to do their own thing.

Hurried lives lead to fatigue, fatigue leads to irritability, and irritability leads to isolation. If assault or ambush is involved in the mix, anger or anxiety isn't far behind. That causes any isolation to accelerate into aloneness with painful consequences.

Brittle Souls and Spiritual Longing

It almost seems as if America and the Western world are headed toward an Armageddon of the spirit. Our society seems ready to self-destruct as we turn on each other in our anger, anxiety, and growing aloneness.

If you take time to look up from your own pain, you will notice that we have brokenness and brittle souls everywhere. The silent cries of these broken hearts are deafening.

At the same time, there is a level of spiritual longing in our society that I have never seen before. People everywhere seem to be searching frantically for God. Their attitude is: "You can talk angels, you can talk anything you want, man. I just hope He's there for me."

It shows up in almost every area of modern life. I'm convinced that even our nation's growing fascination with lotteries reflects the search for something more. People who say, "Maybe one day my ship will come in—I pray and keep buying my Lotto tickets every week just in case" are really reaching toward unblemished bliss every way they can. People who say, "I want to be touched by angels. I want to hear them. I want to believe that they are around me," are really saying, "I want to believe there is a God who loves me."

That is the problem—even among born-again Christians! Most of us don't *really* believe that God loves us!

✦ *Most of us don't* really *believe that God loves us!*

"I'm too far gone, there's too much water under the bridge. He can't love me." Nearly all of the Christian leaders I have worked with have reached the place where they seriously doubt that God loves them—in fact, they believed God was ashamed of them! This nearly always made them feel very, very alone in life.

When you feel alone with only your anger or your anxiety to comfort you, the sense of safety and security you crave just isn't there anymore.

The Ultimate Escape from Pain

Loneliness is ugly. It hurts the human soul on a massive scale. In fact, loneliness may well be one of the biggest causes of heartbreak among our nation's elderly. Few people know that

America's highest suicide rate is found among men over the age of eighty-five.[3]

I think it is because they come to believe they have lost everything. Many have lost their sense of who they are. Without a sense of identity, you also lose your sense of personal value—and with it, your primary reason for living. For the most desperate, life seems to be nothing but perpetual loss and endless aloneness.

+ *Loneliness hurts the human soul on a massive scale.*

Aloneness eats at your soul. Perhaps that is why God declared it is not good that man be alone. This feeling of aloneness can be one of the most dangerous stages in the downward spiral toward loss of heart. For many, the train stops here in a desperate act of suicide.

We've already mentioned the elderly victims, but the despair of loneliness knows no age boundary. Suicide is a growing problem as our society and governmental institutions flee from God's influence in virtually every area of life.

Suicide may be defined as *the taking of one's life in order to eliminate pain.* It is nothing less than the tragic and lethal culmination of unresolved events that created depression and hopelessness.

Someone considering suicide sees no hope that the future will be different than his painful past or present. (Ironically, the risk of suicide is greatest within the first year after a failed attempt.)

Males tend to use more violent means for suicide (guns, cars) and are more often successful than women. But females tend to attempt suicide more often than men but are less often successful at the attempt because they use less-lethal means (such as pills or cutting themselves).

✦ *Anyone having suicidal thoughts is in genuine crisis—he needs my love and the love of God.*

Suicidal individuals suffer from tunnel vision. They do not see any option except death, so to them suicide is simply a logical thing to do. That helps explain why suicidal individuals sometimes end up taking the lives of others as they kill themselves—they do not see the big picture.

For all of these reasons, we should always take seriously the threat of suicide. When I talk with people who are suicidal, I don't contradict them or try to get all their thinking to match up with God's Word—that isn't the time for it.

Anyone having suicidal thoughts is in genuine crisis—he needs my love and the love of God more than he needs to be pounded with correct theology in that moment. (Since suicide is essentially illogical, nothing I could say would argue him out of how he feels. He must be *loved* out of his pain.)

While some Christians may resist suicide because they believe it is a sin, such rules are often meaningless to those with tunnel vision (and this often includes those suffering the effects of severe loneliness). Although the idea that God loves them may comfort those who feel discouraged or sad, suicidal people are often too depressed to believe it. Severe depression often develops in a life season marked by assault, anger, anxiety, and loneliness!

If you are in this dark place, please understand that the very existence of this book—and the remarkable fact that somehow you are reading these words in this moment—amounts to incredible proof of God's gracious love for you.

You matter to God, and you matter to me and many others besides. Don't give up! There is always hope with God![4]

If you are suicidal, please, immediately:

+ Call 911 or go to an emergency room.
+ Call 1-800-SUICIDE, a twenty-four-hour hot line for persons battling suicide, or look for a hot line in your local area in the phone book.
+ Call a trusted friend, pastor, or mental health professional. *Don't* try to cope with this feeling all alone.

You *Do* Have Purpose

Many people who feel desperately alone will tell you, "I've lost my sense of purpose." That is because purpose flows out of love. The Bible says: "For the love of Christ controls us, having concluded this, that one died for all, therefore all died; and He died for all, that they who live might no longer live for themselves, but for Him who died and rose again on their behalf" (2 Cor. 5:14–15 NASB).

We lose our sense of direction and purpose when we feel unloved or rejected because of broken relationships with God and man. We may think, *What is my role? I just don't know anymore. I don't fit in. That's all there is.*

Some of the pressure comes from God's purpose-driven people trying to live in a society that measures personal value based on what we do or what others' opinions of us are. Once you are *perceived*—whether it is fact or fiction—to be no longer useful or productive (for instance, if you are elderly or physically or mentally incapacitated), then you are suddenly deemed useless. You are made to feel you are just in the way.

When you buy the lie and begin to feel you are in the way,

your heart cry begins to sound hauntingly like that of Job in the midst of his pain: "I would rather die of strangulation than go on and on like this. I hate my life. I do not want to go on living. Oh, leave me alone for these few remaining days. . . . Have I sinned? What have I done to you, O watcher of all humanity? Why have you made me your target? Am I a burden to you?" (Job 7:15–16, 20 NLT).

You begin to empathize with the disheartened cry of Solomon at the height of his sorrow, when hope was gone and he had lost all heart for the fight of life: "I have seen all the works that are done under the sun; and, behold, all is vanity and vexation of spirit. That which is crooked cannot be made straight: and that which is wanting cannot be numbered" (Eccl. 1:14–15 KJV).

The New Living Translation (NLT) restates Ecclesiastes 1:15 this way: "What is wrong cannot be righted. What is missing cannot be recovered." Remember that Solomon was truthfully expressing his despair, but *it was not necessarily the truth*. In the same way, Elijah the prophet, who had faced down pagan priests in a miraculous trial by fire, also found himself crying out, "I, even I only, am left; and they seek my life, to take it away" (1 Kings 19:14 KJV). But he wasn't. God was at work.

By this stage of the journey to the loss of heart, your aloneness has become a force to be reckoned with. It not only keeps *you* away from others; it now moves into a new level of power in your life: it begins to *drive others* away from *you*!

Questions for Discussion and Reflection

1. Describe what it is like to be alone, or to feel all alone in the world.

2. Can you remember a time when you were tempted to believe that *Yes, God is good. He's just not good to* me?
3. It is when we are alone that we begin to believe that life isn't fair, that life is unkind. What part of your life seems most unfair or unkind right now?
4. In your despair, who do you think would empathize best with you: Job, Solomon, or Elijah—or all three of them?

Action Point: If you feel enveloped in aloneness, seek out just one person today with whom you feel safe. Ask that person to pray with you and for you. Arrange to meet weekly, or more often if needed. And don't forget that God is as near as your prayer for help.

CRUISING ON
ALIENATION HIGHWAY
Hurting and Headed for a Breakdown

Hardship can thrust you onto the slippery path toward loss of heart and vault you through anger, anxiety, aloneness, and then, alienation.

None of these is the final destination of the journey to the loss of heart, but each one can feel like it. That final destination is an emotional and spiritual abyss where you feel estranged from everyone. It is where evil voices whisper lies that dilute every hope of a better life.

Here you feel *alienated* from virtually every person in your life, and at the same time others' relationships with you can suffer as well. It is *aloneness on the family plan*, or *relational separation with a group discount*.

When you feel alienated, you feel people doing more than merely distancing themselves from you. They are out to get you. You are convinced they want to hurt or hinder you in some way. For this reason, you are rarely the most pleasant person at the party. Anyone brave enough to approach you—family members, friends, coworkers, and even your counselor—may feel as if he or she is trying to snuggle up to a porcupine with a hangover.

The net result of alienation is division. It is separation from all that matters the most to you. Remember, you were made for relationship. When you feel alienated, you start cutting yourself off from your most vital, life-giving relationships. Your journey looks like this:

Losing Heart: The Descent into Pain
Ambushed and Assaulted
Anger
Anxiety
Aloneness
Alienation

At the same time, you sow seeds of despair in your life and the lives of those who care about you the most. When we fail to solve our problems at this stage, they really start to snowball because that failure leads to another "double-A" response: *alienation* and its companion response, *arrogance*. (We define arrogance and deal with its implications in the next chapter.)

In the Alienation Stage, You Rapidly Separate Yourself

Remember:

+ When you feel angry, you go *against* people.

✦ When you feel anxious, you begin to *pull inward,* away from people.

✦ When you feel alone, you begin to *withdraw from people altogether.*

✦ When you feel alienated, you *feel everyone is against you*— and your extremely defensive feelings begin to affect others.

This is life's hard edge. It makes you feel so broken and hurt that you can't hear anymore. You are desperate to fix what isn't right, and when everything else fails you pull in and feel pushed away. Alienation is essentially a form of raw desperation.

✦ *Alienation is essentially a form of raw desperation.*

One preacher felt so driven to "seek and save the lost" with the gospel of hope that he neglected his most important personal relationships. As he felt more and more alone, his alienation began to deafen him to the cries of those he loved.

After dinner and prayer, this busy pastor announced to his boys, "I've got to go on visitation tonight." Alone and dejected because of Dad's busyness, the pastor's fifteen-year-old son looked across the table and said, "Hey Dad, why don't you visit *us?*"

Do you know what that pastor did? *He went on visitation anyway!* Alienation had blocked him from hearing the voice of God thundering through the wounded words of his angry teenage son!

We would all assume that in his spiritual position, this dedicated pastor would be eager to receive God's messages. But even when the Spirit of God is working, it is almost as if the victim of alienation can't hear at all.

Alienation is especially devastating to marriage relationships. It sabotages communication and makes reconciliation difficult at best.

What happens when a woman feels her husband doesn't care about her or the children? She says, "All he ever does is come home and sink into his chair. He rarely even looks up to acknowledge our existence." What about the husband who feels alienated by his wife's constant nagging about the house and how much she hates being cooped up? He doesn't feel cared for. When he comes home, he is tired from a hard day's work and he feels alone. Privately, he wonders where the woman he married went to. She used to run to him when he came through the door.

It is as if we've never heard the words "I love you" or registered their meaning. Feelings of alienation essentially close communication channels so that we don't receive anymore. It easily spreads to our children, our church friends, or even to our friends at the workplace.

Alienation Causes You to Suspect and Push Away Others

When you get anxious and fearful around other people, they begin to feel anxious and fearful too! When you become alienated from others, they begin to feel alienated from you as well. So if you move away, they will move away from you. Alienation is the cancer of pain afflicting our most vital relationships.

✦ *Alienation is the cancer of pain afflicting*
our most vital relationships.

Think about it: do *you* like to be around depressed people? The more you alienate yourself, the more the people around you begin to disengage from you. This, in turn, only increases the discouragement that fuels the depression. Depression leads to despair. And despair is loss of heart, or disaffection with God.

For many Christians struggling with the unkind blows and bruises of life, the symptoms of alienation often show up in disappointment. At first we may focus on ourselves or on others, but eventually—perhaps because we often place false expectations on God—we direct our blame at Him.

The book *The Healing Path* described how one man's wounds robbed him of his memory of God's goodness:

> John struggled with trusting God. When he first got fired, he was angry with his boss and the man's inability to see what John's cost-saving measures might produce for the company. After a few weeks, his anger turned against God for not protecting him against the duplicity of his firm. The wound robbed him of his memory of how God had redeemed him, introduced him to his wife, and provided for his son after a near-fatal accident. Refusing to think about anything but the recent betrayal, John's memory of God became clouded.[1]

Once you get to this address in the state of alienation, you almost unconsciously begin to wall off your emotions. You miss all of the cries around you. Worst of all, you can easily miss the call of God, even when He whispers your name.

Hurt and Headed Down the Wrong Road

I told one group of pastors I knew to be suffering from alien-ation, "Some of you have reached the place where your hearts have closed off. You are so tired that you can't even hear God speaking to you right now!"

Shock hit the pastors as if an earthquake had rattled the room. It was visible. Those words had become the arrows of God pricking their hearts. The conviction of the Holy Spirit was almost a tangible thing.

"I'm serious!" I said. "You don't even hear anymore. You are bitter. In fact, you are filled with bitterness. I suspect some of you are so angry right now that you can't even see anymore. I'm telling you that you are destined for a breakdown, and God is going to let you go there too!"

Please understand that I almost *never* talk like that to pas-tors—or to anyone else. But when the Holy Spirit speaks, I have to obey. I've learned that destinies are on the line when I'm dealing with people who feel alienated from everything that matters most in life.

✦ *Destinies are on the line when I'm dealing with people who feel alienated from everything that matters most in life.*

The sad fact is that once we are hurting and headed for a breakdown, we usually have to go all the way. We may have to hit bottom to finally turn around and change direction.

On the Alienation Highway, you will find yourself saying things like, "I don't *need* anybody, I don't *want* anybody, and I definitely can't *trust* anybody anymore, so I'm opting out."

You weren't made for that. God made you to be "a vessel

for honor, sanctified, useful to the Master, prepared for every good work" (2 Tim. 2:21 NASB). Paul gave us a serious warning that especially applies to any of us who have settled into a state of alienation: "If you think you are standing strong, be careful, for you, too, may fall into the same sin" (1 Cor. 10:12 NLT).

It seems as if the bad news accelerates, and the slide toward the loss of heart really begins to spin out of control as you cruise down Alienation Highway. We're destined for a breakdown—dead ahead.

This Is the Sound of Brokenness

Do you know what brokenness sounds like? Are you saying some of these things now?

+ No one understands me, and they don't care anyway! All they want to do is get me out of the way so they can put their favorite in my place. Why did I ever take this job in the first place? I don't know what I'll do, but I'm not playing their game.

+ She doesn't care. All she's after is life the way she wants it—well, I don't want any part of it. I've been hurt for the last time. I don't even feel like part of this family anymore. Even the kids treat me like a stranger.

+ All those years I spent helping those people, and *this* is what I get? They're probably checking out new preachers right now. It doesn't matter how many times they call— I'm not wasting my breath trying to talk to those people. They've already made up their minds. It's only a matter of time: they want me out, they'll get me out. What can I do? *Nothing*. What's the use?

This is the sound of brokenness; that's all it is. It is one of the countless ways a wounded soul screams out, "It's not the way it's supposed to be, and I don't know what to do!"

(By the way, we will never hear the true message behind a wounded person's words if we don't listen deeply and act slowly. It is much easier to slam the book closed, write them off as too far gone, and leave the alienated soul to his or her self-made hell. But that is simply *not* the right thing to do.)

Every time I meet wounded or struggling spiritual leaders, my heart goes out to them because they have one of the most difficult tasks on earth. But something else moves me to tears about this. For every shepherd who is crying out, "It's not the way it's supposed to be," there are hundreds of sheep right behind them.

They are begging their shepherd, "Lead us out of our pain. Show us a better way." But you can't *give* well what you don't *do* well. That is one of the driving motivations behind this book: my heart burns to see shepherds and sheep alike living healthy, vibrant lives through the power of Christ and the cross.

When you find yourself living in alienation, you find it virtually irresistible to blame others and suspect the motives of even your closest friends.

View the Devastated Landscape Produced by Uncontrolled Alienation

In the C. S. Lewis classic *The Great Divorce*, Lewis pictures hell and heaven in a particular way to help us understand the devilish nature of bitterness, fear, unforgiveness, manipulative "love," and blame-laying.

In the process, he brilliantly portrays the devastated land-scape produced by uncontrolled alienation in the human soul, where we are constantly becoming more and more separated from others.

Consider this description. The central character, a relatively new arrival who is waiting to take an excursion bus to the outer reaches of heaven, receives this description of "grey town" (or hell) from a longtime resident:

> "It seems the deuce of a town," I volunteered, "and that's what I can't understand. The parts of it that I saw were so empty. Was there once a larger population?"
>
> "Not at all," said my neighbour. "The problem is that they're so quarrelsome. As soon as anyone arrives he settles in some street. Before he's been there twenty-four hours he quarrels with his neighbour. Before the week is over he's quarreled so badly that he decides to move. Very likely he finds the next street empty because all the people there have quarreled with *their* neighbours—and moved."[2]

It seems the earliest arrivals to grey town, including such great sinners and self-centered characters as Genghis Khan, Julius Caesar, and Henry V, so alienated themselves from others that they moved "light years" away to avoid any contact with the rest of hell's residents.

Another familiar historical character seems to illustrate perfectly what it means to be trapped in the state of alienation. Although he was an early arrival, he, too, had migrated light years away from the center of "grey town" in his effort to be alone and apart from any other soul. Here's a conversation between two people who were watching this man:

"We've picked out the house by now. Just a little pin prick of light [in a telescope] and nothing else near it for millions of miles."

"But they got there?"

"That's right. He'd built himself a huge house all in the Empire style—rows of windows flaming with light, though it only shows as a pin prick from where I live."

"Did they see Napoleon?"

"That's right. They went up and looked through one of the windows. Napoleon was there all right."

"What was he doing?"

"Walking up and down—up and down all the time—left-right, left-right—never stopping for a moment. The two chaps watched him for about a year and he never rested. And muttering to himself all the time. 'It was Soult's fault. It was Ney's fault. It was Josephine's fault. It was the fault of the Russians. It was the fault of the English.' Like that all the time. Never stopped for a moment. A little, fat man and he looked kind of tired. But he didn't seem able to stop it."[3]

I've said it before, but I'll say it again: God made us for relationship. It is embedded in His master design for our souls. Here's an example of how true this is: Little babies raised in mass orphanages in some of the Balkan countries under the former Soviet Union were deprived of human touch, interaction, and affection. They received adequate food, were clothed, and were kept out of the elements, but they were raised under a system that denied the existence of the soul.

When Western visitors and members of the media visited these orphanages, they were shocked to find so many of these otherwise normal children exhibiting severe forms of mental retardation, learning delays, or complete social breakdown.

We know from the Scriptures that in Christ, life *is* supposed to be different now. It may not be trouble free, but it should be different.

* Therefore if any man be in Christ, he is a new creature: old things are passed away; behold, all things are become new. (2 Corinthians 5:17 KJV)
* But you are a chosen generation, a royal priesthood, a holy nation, His own special people, that you may proclaim the praises of Him who called you out of darkness into His marvelous light. (1 Peter 2:9)
* The one who loves his brother abides in the Light and there is no cause for stumbling in him. But the one who hates his brother is in the darkness and walks in the darkness, and does not know where he is going because the darkness has blinded his eyes. (1 John 2:10–11 NASB)
* For our citizenship is in heaven, from which also we eagerly wait for a Savior, the Lord Jesus Christ. (Philippians 3:20 NASB)

As I've pointed out before, Paul was saying, "If you are born from above, if you are really a citizen of heaven, make sure your conduct reflects your citizenship."

When life hurts, we can feel as if our pain is consuming us. On Alienation Highway, you begin to lose your capacity to trust others. It is easier to jump to a conclusion that matches your pain than withhold judgment until the facts are in. Your overblown response might be: "Who are *you* to tell me that? I can't believe it—you are intentionally trying to hurt me! What happened to all the trust you keep talking about? I just don't have time to waste on this garbage. You are wrong about me. In fact, you're wrong about everything. Just leave me alone. We have nothing to talk about."

You Can't Feel, You Can't Trust, and You Don't Hear

At the height of alienation, you can't feel, you can't trust, and you don't hear the cries of hurting people around you. You are oblivious to every attempt to communicate or reconcile—even the attempts made by lifelong friends and family members.

My heart breaks for the frustrated and frightened woman who sees her husband in every description of the alienation stage. I've heard many of them pour out their fears in my office. "He just can't hear anymore. When I try to talk to him, I feel like I'm talking to the wall! He can't even pray. He can't do *anything*."

At the pinnacle of alienation, you seemingly lose all capacity to hear God's voice persistently whispering your name. Yet He is calling. He sees the enormous potential in you.

Nearly every challenge in your life brings you to a fork in your life journey. What choices will you make?

Will you surrender to your pain and submit to the pressures of life, or will you follow Christ through the valley of the loss of heart? Will you trust Him until you ascend to full recovery of your heart and come out of your pain?

God Never Tires!

Let me inject some bright hope right here.

What's so beautiful about God is that even in the face of our alienation and unlovely attempts to separate ourselves from Him, *He never tires!* Charles Spurgeon described the persistence of Satan in his evil deeds: "There is nothing that Satan can do for his evil cause that he does not do. We may be half-

hearted but he never is. He is the very image of ceaseless industry and untiring earnestness. He will do all that can be done in
the time of his permitted rage. We may be sure that he will
never lose a day."[4]

The good news is that God won't either. And He has already
done all that can be done to set us free from every sin or problem in life! Jesus did it all on the cross. The Bible couldn't make
it any clearer:

+ And [Jesus] said unto them, I beheld Satan as lightning
  fall from heaven. Behold, I give unto you power . . . over
  all the power of the enemy: and nothing shall by any
  means hurt you. (Luke 10:18–19 KJV)
+ At the name of Jesus every knee should bow, of things in
  heaven, and things in earth, and things under the earth;
  that that every tongue should confess that Jesus Christ
  is Lord, to the glory of God the Father. (Philippians
  2:10–11 KJV)

We still face the devastation of genuine pain in our Christian
lives right now. Many times we find our lives disintegrating
when we respond to assaults with anger and anxiety, followed
by aloneness and then devastating feelings of alienation.

I am convinced that even in your alienation, even if you are
living in rebellion right now, God will keep knocking. The real
problems come when you keep tuning out the voice of the
Holy Spirit. It is as if you've got your fist clenched and your
spirit shut down just so you won't hear Him calling you back
to Himself.

+ *God will keep knocking.*

The slippery slope is turning into a slippery chute. A long fall is ahead, and the loss of heart is the only thing you have to look forward to at the bottom.

If you are so alienated from God that you can't or won't see or hear Him anymore, then, as I said earlier, you are destined for a breakdown.

Questions for Discussion and Reflection

1. Have you alienated yourself from others? Do you presently feel as if everyone is against you?
2. Have you found yourself saying things like, "I don't need anybody, I don't want anybody, and I definitely can't trust anybody anymore"?
3. What are your natural defenses when you feel this way?
4. Have those closest to you in your life ever confronted you about your distancing yourself? Did you ever find that you hurt somebody close to you because you alienated yourself?
5. Do you find others distancing themselves from you?
6. Do you trust the Lord to lead you through the valley of the loss of heart? Will you trust Him until you ascend to full recovery of your heart?

Action Point: Refuse to accept the lie that everyone is against you. Look for supportive Scriptures about God's nearness and desire to help (such as Ps. 23; Isa. 41:10–13; Ps. 86; Rom. 8:26–27, 31–39). Call on Him and at least one person you trust. Confess your struggle and ask for help.

ARROGANCE ON PARADE
A Porcupine Is Loose in the House!

The internal blame game that bloomed in your alienation stage has now become a very clearly communicated *external* expression, which only adds to your problems. When you reach the *arrogance* stage, you find being around others piercingly *painful*.

If we use as an analogy the onset stage of chicken pox or mumps to your feelings, then your increasing feelings of brokenness are like full-blown blisters and extremely swollen lymph glands that give outward and visible proof to the virus of pain within.

Here your journey looks like this:

Losing Heart: The Descent into Pain
Ambushed and Assaulted

Anger
Anxiety
Aloneness
Alienation
Arrogance

What's sad about the arrogance stage is that the wounded one is beginning to wound others—and even drive away healers and comforters. It isn't that you are arrogant per se. You are *perceived* to be arrogant when you are really lost in a deepened preoccupation with your pain. You have become completely absorbed with a life that is not the way it is supposed to be, and in the process you become nearsighted and unable to hear or receive effectively from others.

Other people see you as aloof and preoccupied. It makes sense, doesn't it? Even God struggles to get your attention at this stage. Even now, as He reaches toward your heart, is it closed? Do you just press on, thinking, *I guess I'll just have to go it alone?*

✦ *Do you just press on, thinking,*
I guess I'll just have to go it alone?

Alienation and arrogance virtually dominated the sad life of King Saul, as it is described in the book of 1 Samuel. Once the pride and joy of his people, Israel's first king stood head and shoulders above his brethren. Saul enjoyed a reputation as a valiant warrior and popular leader. He was handsome and charismatic, and he seemed just humble enough on the outside to appeal to the masses. Then his nearsighted view of God, his playing the blame game, and his overblown estimate of his own worth took a fatal turn:

And Saul said to Samuel, "But I have obeyed the voice of the LORD, and gone on the mission on which the Lord sent me, and brought back Agag king of Amalek; I have utterly destroyed the Amalekites. But *the people* took of the plunder, sheep and oxen, the best of the things which should have been utterly destroyed, to sacrifice to the LORD your God in Gilgal."

So Samuel said,

"Has the LORD as great delight in burnt offerings and
    sacrifices,
As in obeying the voice of the LORD?
Behold, to obey is better than sacrifice,
And to heed than the fat of rams.
For rebellion is as the sin of witchcraft,
And stubbornness is as iniquity and idolatry.
Because you have rejected the word of the LORD,
He also has rejected you from being king."

Then Saul said to Samuel, "I have sinned, for I have transgressed the commandment of the LORD and your words, because I feared the people and obeyed their voice."

(1 Samuel 15:20–24, emphasis mine)

Saul's greatest problems were self-inflicted. He chose to please the people instead of obeying God, and Samuel the prophet predicted that God would give Saul's kingdom to another. The virus of anxiety must have taken root at that point, and for good reason—God had lifted His hand from Saul's life.

As the years went by, in Saul's eyes the greatest disaster of his life wasn't his loss of favor with God; it was a skinny, unknown country kid named David. King Saul's greatest public relations problem prior to David's entrance on the national scene was a pesky giant named Goliath, who had single-handedly silenced and shamed Saul's army. He had made it his goal to publicly humiliate King Saul.

When the youngster named David showed up and managed to remove Goliath's head in dramatic fashion, King Saul was quick to lavish gratitude and honor on the teenager as only a king can. All was well until King Saul overheard his fans giving more honor to the kid than to their king. From the moment of this psychological assault until his death many years later, jealous fear, anger, and anxiety seemed to haunt Saul's waking hours. The Bible says,

> It had happened as they were coming home, when David was returning from the slaughter of the Philistine, that the women had come out of all the cities of Israel, singing and dancing, to meet King Saul, with tambourines, with joy, and with musical instruments. So the women sang as they danced, and said:
>
> > "Saul has slain his thousands,
> > And David his ten thousands."
>
> Then Saul was very angry, and the saying displeased him; and he said, "They have ascribed to David ten thousands, and to me they have ascribed only thousands. Now what more can he have but the kingdom?" So Saul eyed David from that day forward.
>
> (1 Samuel 18:6–9)

Saul's Alienation Quickly Turned to Arrogance

After David's triumph, internal turmoil nearly consumed Saul. The king's alienation quickly moved to the *arrogance* stage as the outflow of Saul's internal pain began to take on deadly external forms. The only relief he found early in the process was in the anointed music of David. Yet the very sight and sound of his nemesis so close by nearly drove Saul mad. On more than one occasion, he threw a javelin at David: "And it happened on the next day that the distressing spirit from God came upon Saul, and he prophesied inside the house. So David played music with his hand, as at other times; but there was a spear in Saul's hand. And Saul cast the spear, for he said, 'I will pin David to the wall!' But David escaped his presence twice" (1 Sam. 18:10–11).

This is a very extreme (and possibly psychotic) form of *arrogance on parade*!

When arrogance takes the lead over alienation, the focus turns from *your internal feelings* of alienation to their *external effect* and the *reactions of others* to the new grumpy porcupine in the house.

The hypervigilance that began to set in earlier in the alienation stage now becomes more prominent. Extreme defensiveness begins to run over people on a regular basis.

You might ask, why does a little extra grumpiness make such a big difference? It does because when you are neck-deep in the arrogant stage, calling this behavior "a little extra grumpiness" is like calling skin cancer a "bad rash" that will go away on its own.

Dr. Charles Stanley explained what happens in our lives when the "oil" of healthy, godly character disappears.

> Character is to relationships what oil is to a motor. If you took apart the engine of a new car, you would find that each part was made to work perfectly with all the other parts of that engine. Yet if you run that engine without oil, certain parts of the engine will eventually destroy the parts around them. Why? Friction and heat.

The same is true in relationships. When there is a deficit in character, you pay for it in relationships. It doesn't matter how perfectly suited you are to your spouse, your job, or your club. If you don't have character, there is going to be friction.[1]

"Friction and heat": that is a perfect description of the environment produced by a good person struggling with brokenness and immersed in alienated arrogance.

How You Seem to Others

As the progression of frustration continues in your life, less and less seems to be in your control, and more and more of the time you seem to come across wrong to others.

You don't have a bad heart, because you're not a bad person. But something is going on inside of you that is very wrong. Over time, you've grown deaf to the communication of others—it doesn't matter whether they try to give you good news, bad news, helpful information, or cuss you out. They simply don't penetrate the protective walls around your heart.

People think you're arrogant and self-centered because of your one-sided communication style, but you aren't arrogant in the normal sense of the word. You are so broken inside that you are unnaturally preoccupied with the *why* behind it, and you are searching for any way of escape.

Your mind is rigidly focused on the problem—you want to make sense out of your life. Now, in an odd twist, the people around you are beginning to believe you are simply selfish. They now borrow the internal "alienation script" you've been using and turn it on *you*! When they see you, they may begin to tell you, "All you are concerned is about you." When they talk among themselves, they begin to say, "He doesn't care for us" and "She's just not there for me anymore."

The full effect of alienation turned to arrogance is at work, and all it does is fuel disengagement. A brooding, reinforced sense of aloneness seems to settle like a dark cloud over everything in your personal universe. You feel you are backed into a corner, and you just try to protect yourself. Unfortunately, you come across as just another crank in the corner snarling at life.

Whether or not you have words to describe your wounds, the way you feel is crystal clear: you just can't bear the pain of suffering even one more soul wound.

Part of what happens to you in the state of arrogance is that because you don't feel you can trust anybody, you start crying out in pretended independence, "I don't need anybody!"

✦ *Unfortunately, you come across as just another crank in the corner snarling at life.*

I say those cries are pretended because your words essentially represent a false front, an aggressively defensive line that disguises the truth—you are really crying out for somebody to help. You're just afraid.

You Use Words to Create Distance

It reminds me of all the men I've known who avoided going to the doctor for years—even when they suspected something was wrong. There were actually little boys under those mature exteriors (this is true for most males). Despite all of their life experiences and hard-won wisdom, they still feared the unknown, the frightening possibility of feeling pain or receiving unwelcome news in the office of the white-coated physicians.

The truth is that the best course for them is to give up the myth carried over from youth, the false security that says, "I am invincible. I will live forever." Only then can they face their fears and find the facts. John Eldredge said, "The true test of a man, the beginning of his redemption, actually starts when he can no longer rely on what he's used all his life. The real journey begins when the false self fails."[2]

That is what is behind the harsh words of the husband wrestling with the demons of alienation and arrogance. Rather than receive his wife's attempt to penetrate his walls, he lashes out aggressively with offensive words calculated to put distance between potential pain and his own tortured heart: "You know what? I don't want to talk to you. I don't want to look at you, and I don't want sex from you. I don't want *anything* from you!"

The sad truth is that he is begging for intimacy and reconnection with his wife. He knows there is healing in her love, but he is so angry, so frustrated, and so alienated that *he wounds her* with his words.

Now there are two wounded souls who can't bear to risk the potential pain of trying to reconnect again. The risk required to save the marriage is seen as rapidly outweighing any potential value or hope of success.

When the defensive aggression of arrogance sets in on your soul, you just don't hear when your wife cries and says, "Honey, please. Let's stop fighting." If she gets a response, it is an emotional artillery shell meant to drive back the "enemy": "Quit trying to play games with me."

Arrogance Leads
to Spiritual Insensitivity

Great Christian leaders today who find themselves joining the Arrogance Parade suddenly discover they have become Eli, the spiritually numb priest in Samuel's day. When God called to Samuel and he mistook the voice for Eli's, the priest said, "Samuel, just go back to bed. God doesn't speak anymore—least of all to you. Go away. I've got my own problems to think about."

God wasn't speaking to Eli very much in those days because the aged priest had begun to prefer his sinful sons over God's will. He had grown used to a life in which he didn't hear God's voice or perceive His presence. So Samuel had to approach Eli three times before the old priest realized that God was actually speaking to his young protégé (see 1 Sam. 3:1–8).

You can be a great religious leader and still lose what is most valuable to you. Your sons can be living like the devil right in front of you (and the congregation) and you won't even see it.

Many times, spiritual leaders add another dangerous component to the state of arrogance—they refuse help on the basis of false spiritual pride. Even as they pull their emotions in and drive their families and ministries out, they'll tell you, "All I need is God." What they are really saying is, "I'll just get through this on my own."

We weren't made for that. Whether you are a spiritual leader or not, if you are lashing out at others in your pain, you are dying inside and you don't even know it. It is important to emphasize what is really in the heart of people stuck in the arrogance stage. Otherwise, we will be tempted to lash back at them in self-defense.

> ✦ *All of our braggadocio and brave defiance are*
> *just a front for how we really feel: "God, help me!"*

All of our braggadocio and brave defiance are just a front for how we really feel: "God, help me! I'm dying here. I know I'm over my head, and I know I'm treating people harshly—I don't even like myself right now! Will somebody break through these walls and rescue me?"

Jesus said, "Out of the abundance of the heart the mouth speaketh" (Matt. 12:34 KJV). What pours out of our hearts in the arrogance stage is a toxic mixture of anger, anxiety, confusion, discouragement, accusation, pleading, and endless justification for stinking thinking.

Thank God for His loving mercies! We should be glad they are renewed every morning! (Lam. 3:22–23).

The Birth of Clinical Depression

Let me warn you that aloneness, alienation, and arrogance are where clinical depression can begin to take root. And I'm talking about something far more serious and painful than a temporary dose of the blues.

Depression isn't something you snap out of on your own. It aggravates your levels of anger and anxiety, and the more depressed you are, the more prickly you are.

Sadness differs from depression in that sadness is a God-given reaction to loss that serves to slow us down so we may process grief. When we are sad, self-respect remains intact, intrinsic hope is alive, we experience relief after crying, and we readily seek out others for support.

If alienation and arrogance birth depression, it stands to reason we might also carry some of their symptoms and characteristics into the depressive state. One of those is the avoidance of others—even to our own hurt.

The frequency of depression is on the rise. Whether depression is classified as an illness, syndrome, disorder, or disease, it is estimated up to 20 percent of the U.S. population suffers from clinical depression at any given time.[3]

People born after 1950 are ten times as likely to experience depression as compared to their predecessors! People between the ages of twenty-five and forty-five suffer depression the most, but it is ominous that adolescent groups possess the fastest rate of depression *growth*.[4]

The problem of depression produces pain for both the victims of the disorder and those closest to the sufferers. Unfortunately, most sufferers do not seek treatment or believe their depression to be a treatable illness.[5]

The Bible is filled with vivid examples of depression:

- ✦ David described his depression caused by sin (Ps. 38).
- ✦ God used depression to get Nehemiah's attention (Neh.1–2).
- ✦ Job's devastating losses led him to curse the day he was born (Job 1–3).
- ✦ Elijah was so depressed he wished to die (1 Kings 19:4).

The symptoms of clinical depression include decreased energy, fluctuating body weight, inability to concentrate, irritability, bouts of crying, despair, lack of interest in pleasurable activities, social withdrawal, and thoughts of suicide.

Psalm 102 provides an effective checklist of depression symptoms a psalmist displayed.

+ "Do not hide your face from me in the day of trouble" (v. 2). *God just doesn't hear my prayers anymore.*
+ "For my days are consumed like smoke, and my bones are burned like a hearth" (v. 3). *It's all gone in a flash—my life is over! My bones just ache over all this.*
+ "My heart is stricken and withered like grass, / So that I forget to eat my bread" (v. 4). *I just don't know if I can recover from this. I don't have the heart to try. I can't even eat anymore—I can't remember the last time I was hungry. . . .*
+ "Because of the sound of my groaning / My bones cling to my skin" (v. 5). *I just stay up all night, crying in the dark. I've lost so much weight I can see my bones through the skin.*
+ "I lie awake, / And am like a sparrow alone on the housetop" (v. 7). *I feel as if I've been removed from the merry-go-round of life, stuck on a rooftop somewhere, and sentenced to watch helplessly as the world goes by without any notice of my absence or aloneness. I don't think I care anyway—it's their loss and my gain. Who needs 'em?*
+ "My enemies reproach me all day long; / Those who deride me swear an oath against me" (v. 8). *I used to think they were my friends, but all they do is put me down. I don't even know why I go to work anymore. They've all decided: I'm out, and they're in.*
+ "For I have eaten ashes like bread, / And mingled my drink with weeping" (v. 9). *Everything I eat tastes like burnt toast, and I can't even take a drink without tears falling into it.*
+ ". . . Because of Your indignation and Your wrath; For You have lifted me up and cast me away" (v. 10). *Even God seems to be mad at me! He used to take care of me, but I think He dropped me in favor of other people who aren't as messed up.*
+ "My days are like a shadow that lengthens, / And I wither

away like grass" (v. 11). *I can't put my finger on it, but somewhere in my past my day in the sun began to end, and I didn't even know it. It's sad. I feel as if I'm dying and nobody I know can even begin to understand. I wonder if any of them really care.*

When life in the fast lane of arrogance produces no improvement, you inevitably find yourself spiraling down into yet another place of even greater pain—it is a place of wandering and experimenting with "lesser gods."

When Attempts at Self-Preservation Actually Destroy

It would be best to stop the downward spiral right here, but few people make a successful stand in this stage. When you are convinced that you don't need anyone, then it is easy to say, "No, I don't need counseling. I'll handle this myself. Nobody could understand anyway, so why should I let somebody I don't know peel back my memories? Every time I've tried to let people in, all I got was hurt more."

The over-the-top defensive tactics and offensive responses we see in the arrogance stage are really acts of self-preservation. Despite that, intervention is needed because emotional suicide is taking root!

Another even more sinister stage in this spiraling descent into pain awaits us—I call it *adulteries of the heart.*

✦ *Intervention is needed because
emotional suicide is taking root!*

Questions for Discussion and Reflection

1. What are the characteristics and behaviors of arrogance? When you see it in others, what do you see?
2. Have you ever appeared arrogant to others? Has anybody ever told you such?
3. Have you slid behind false spiritual pride, saying, "God is all I need" when all along you're really saying, "I can do this on my own"?
4. Where do you turn when others are distancing themselves from you?
5. Do you trust God is there for you? Do you believe He is powerful enough to help you out? Are you willing to let Him?

Action Point: If someone has told you that you are arrogant, stop for a moment and consider the accusation. Is there a grain of truth in what that person said? See if someone you know loves you will help you discern whether arrogance has taken root. Confess any sins and describe your struggle to God. If you can stop the downward spiral now, you will save yourself much heartache.

· 7 ·

ADULTERIES OF THE HEART
Replacing God with Trivial Pursuits

The sheer effort of trying to live on the shifting slopes of a volcano can make you feel exhausted and empty. Imagine trying to sleep when the thunder of imminent explosion constantly roars in your ears and rocks every cell of your body.

Anyone who has flown into Guatemala City, the capital of Guatemala, may have some inkling of risky living at its nervous best. Almost any photograph you take will show a saw-toothed horizon, because that city is literally ringed with sharp-tipped, *active* volcanoes! Smoke or steam is almost always rising from some of those volcanoes, and you don't need binoculars to confirm it. If you look very long or very closely at that active volcanic backdrop, sleep may not come easily during your visit to that vast city.

What would it be like waking, living, and sleeping over unseen but active fires—never knowing when the very ground under your feet will erupt and cast you into oblivion? It would be like living with the internal pressures of growing alienation and arrogance. It is simply the way of life in perpetual crisis.

The problem is that you just can't stay in a state of crisis for very long. Your body will die prematurely, your mind will snap, or your nervous system will simply shut down in the interest of self-preservation.

When the causes of our crises remain unhealed and unresolved, our dissatisfaction only grows in intensity and urgency.

✦ *Many a good person has turned to something else—any-*thing else—*in a desperate bid to satisfy the aching emptiness of the soul.*

Our Flight to Outside Comforts

The painful journey through anger, anxiousness, and the ache of aloneness is tough enough. But life becomes unbearable with the digression into alienation and arrogance. For men and women caught in this spiral, even the relationships they could always count on may become so damaged in their personal meltdown process that they find themselves with nowhere to turn.

Cornered, distanced, and despairing, many a good person has turned to something else—*anything else*—in a desperate bid to satisfy the aching emptiness of the soul. Your journey looks like this:

Losing Heart: The Descent into Pain
Ambushed and Assaulted

Anger
Anxiety
Aloneness
Alienation
Arrogance
Adulteries of the Heart

Early on, our flight to outside comforts in this *adulteries of the heart* phase feels good—but those feelings of soothing calmness are only passing illusions.

The "drugs" of choice we turn to at this point—food, pornography, workaholism, alcohol, narcotics, or a lover—offer a measure of comfort and distraction we can hide behind. Sadly, such temporary affairs with empty idols can never fulfill the deepest longings of the heart.

When ministering on the subject of grief, I often mention an old friend of mine with whom I played a lot of baseball in the early days. When his little girl was about four, she came down with a virulent fever that took her life in less than forty-eight hours.

She was his baby girl, the joy of his life, and her death literally broke his heart. I can still see him bending over that tiny casket, taking his little girl's body in his arms and pulling that lifeless face close so he could kiss her one last time. I'll never forget the pain that poured from his ruptured soul that day.

Sometimes, life just isn't fair and no logical explanation is good enough. When you get to the place that anger overtakes reason, nothing makes sense, and descent into even deeper pain is brutal and sudden.

In Search of Fullness, Wholeness, and Restoration

Emptiness seeks fullness. Brokenness longs for wholeness. Exhaustion seeks restoration. In pain, confusion, anger, and alienation, we begin to search for *anything* to make our pain go away—even if only for a brief moment. We're desperate to slake our thirst, even if every swallow moves us closer to the end.

꜅

The faithful wife, mother, and Sunday school teacher finds herself so broken over the loss of her husband to the secretary (who was thirty pounds lighter, twenty years younger, and several shades blonder than she)—stalled for an hour before she finally got out of her car and entered the corner liquor store just before closing time.

The clerk noticed her uncertainty. When he asked what she was looking for, her only reply, given in an oddly disconnected voice, was, "The strongest. Give me the strongest thing you have. No, give me two of them."

꜅

The site just came up out of nowhere the first time, and the corporate officer deleted it, wondering how *that* made it through the computer department's filtering systems.

A week later, after two all-nighters and a grueling audit triggered by unfounded allegations of misappropriation of funds—and the latest of a long series of fights with his wife—he couldn't shake the lurid images he saw in that brief encounter. Glancing around quickly, he accessed his browser's history files and jotted down the site address.

That night—after their final fight, when he and his frustrated wife returned to their corners in different parts of the house—he crossed the line into the forbidden zone in the privacy of his home office.

For three hours he forgot about his broken relationship with the woman who gave birth to their three children. All that night, he wrestled with guilt and sorrow over his secret betrayal and the dirtiness he felt in his soul.

The final game was over, and his selection as all-American fullback and all-state first team was secure. The high school senior slipped away from the team party to his car. In the midst of all the fanfare, he has been disintegrating from the inside out.

Stress from his coaches, unending pressure from his upwardly mobile parents, the grades that secretly threatened his graduation, and the full-ride scholarships: each was taking its toll. Nothing seemed to help—even his best friends were steering clear now. Despite his sports successes, his unexplained moodiness and angry outbursts had made him an untouchable off the field.

Desperate for a break in his secret hell, he quietly acquired a small packet of crystal meth—"It does a body good," or so he'd heard. Just this time, he thought, *just one time to get me by.*

The shock hadn't worn off for the twenty-something graduate student. The wedding gown was still in her closet, the tag still attached; her delicate high-heeled shoes were still unworn and in the original box.

Why did he propose if he didn't intend to follow through? she'd asked herself hundreds of times.

Unable to handle another hour alone in her dreary apartment, she decided to go to the singles bar she passed every day on the way to class. What could it hurt? She'd never been to one, but she deserved a change. She was finished mourning over that jerk! And she was tired of praying about it too.

Too tired to fight her feelings, and too lonely to stay where she was, she picked out a special outfit chosen to capture the eye and headed for the bar.

When she awoke the next morning in the abandoned hotel room, she couldn't remember how she got there. . . .

Trivial Pursuits Chosen to Replace God

When things don't go well despite our best efforts to fix what is broken, we begin seeking other solutions, trivial pursuits to replace the God who has so disappointed us. Like little boys or girls running amok through a hardware store just beyond reach of their parents, we grasp for and touch everything in sight— regardless of whether it poses dangers or not. We are hurting inside and desperate for some relief because life's just not supposed to be this way.

For a time, the booze, the temporary laughter of the easiest friends money can buy, or the stupor induced by chemicals and fatigue seems to offer some brief relief for the unbroken pain of the journey.

Beggars can't be choosers. When you can't get steak, tube steak (hot dogs) will do. When the life of happiness avoids you, perhaps you'll make do with a ninety-minute diversion with a pornographic movie, a four-hour shopping spree with money you don't have, three days of binge and purge, or emptying your saving account at the nearest state-run casino or Internet gambling site.

These are the adulteries of the heart with which we fill our emptiness.

Disordered Affections:
When Life Is All Wrong

We will use them all—temporary, profane, costly, or risky—to anesthetize the pain in our lives. What a bitterly unsatisfying exchange!

These adulteries of the heart can also be called *disordered affections*, where everything is out of sort, priorities are out of whack, and life is all wrong. They produce living nightmares in living color, when a man wakes up too late in his marriage to discover that his kids are gone and his wife has left him. In shock he lifts his bleary eyes to the heavens and cries out, "God, what did I do?"

This is where X marks the spot. You're at a dangerous point of no return, a place that draws you deeper to finish the journey of pain. Feeling overwhelmed and frantic to find "something else," you can't bear to turn outward to seek help from those you love. Instead you turn even more inward and away from your usual sources of comfort. Then begins your pursuit of something else to calm your troubled soul.

This is the spot where doubt is affecting and infecting even your core relational beliefs. Consciously or subconsciously, you aim most of the offense toward God: "If You're not going to be there for me, I'm going to turn away from You and find something else to satisfy my needs." Thus begins the fruitless search for lesser things to satisfy the soul, to fill the hole in your heart, and to anesthetize the relentless, unbearable pain.

In the Bible, this is known as *idolatry*—the fruitless pursuit of anything besides God to fill what only He can fill.

It's My Choice,
and I'll Have What I Want

Now, perhaps we see why Paul could say, "I am terrified lest somehow, as the serpent deceived Eve by his craftiness, so your minds could become corrupted" (see 2 Cor. 11:3). You may think, *There's something between me and Him. It is an offense I just won't release, and I feel unclean. It's something that keeps me from experiencing His abiding presence and His power in my life. But it's my choice, and I'll have what I want (since it can't be God—He just won't bend or try to understand me).*

The classic book *The Problem of Pain* described our hopeless quest to find peace in "false happiness":

> We "have all we want" is a terrible saying when "all" does not include God. . . .
>
> Now God, who has made us, knows what we are and that our happiness lies in Him. Yet we will not seek it in Him as long as He leaves us any other resort where it can even plausibly be looked for.
>
> . . . What then can God do in our interests but make our own life less agreeable to us, and take away the plausible sources of false happiness?[1]

When we indulge in adulteries of the heart, we become curious philanderers striking up sometime encounters and passing romances with whatever pleasure, vice, or hobby seems most likely to satisfy our dissatisfaction (or cover our dysfunction).

✦ *We become curious philanderers striking up*
sometime encounters.

We abuse substances, experiment with forbidden relationships, gamble away our savings in one night, hide behind our clothes, eat to soothe the emptiness, visit the porno shops we used to picket on Sunday afternoons, or surf through pornographic sites on the Internet after the evening news (when everyone else is busy or asleep).

Some of us, in the high name of religion, may impulsively attend every church service and revival we can find, seeking reassurance of our spirituality while leaving behind a wounded spouse and love-starved children to fend for themselves day after day and night after night.

The Usual Suspects: Drugs, Alcohol, and Pornography

The experiment can prove to be a costly one—not that we would care a whit about statistics, principles, warnings, or moral signposts at this stage (we're thinking, *I'm hurting—can't you see that?!*). I provide them nonetheless, especially in the areas of alcohol and drug abuse and pornography, because of their destructive effect on the innocent lives around us:

+ In the year 2000, approximately eighty-five thousand deaths in the U.S. were attributable to either excessive or hazardous drinking—making alcohol the third actual leading cause of death.
+ In 2001, there were 1.4 million arrests for driving under the influence of alcohol or narcotics: that is one out of every 137 licensed drivers.
+ About 80 percent of studies find a positive correlation between drug abuse and personality disorders.

+ Approximately 40 percent of all crimes are committed under the influence of alcohol.

+ Approximately 40 percent of persons convicted of rape or sexual assault state that they were drinking at the time of the offense.

+ As many as 72 percent of rapes on college campuses occur while *victims* are intoxicated to the point where they are unable to consent to or refuse sex.

+ As much as 50 percent of child abuse or neglect cases are connected with the alcohol or drug use of a guardian.[2]

Look at some other sobering statistics:

+ U.S. adults who regularly visit Internet pornography Web sites: 40 million

+ Promise Keeper men who viewed pornography in last week: 53 percent

+ Christians who said pornography is a major problem in the home: 47 percent

+ Average age of first Internet exposure to pornography: eleven years old

+ Kids eight to sixteen who've viewed porn online: 90 percent (most while doing homework)

+ Pornographic Web sites: 4.2 million (12 percent of total Web sites)

+ Daily pornographic search engine requests: 68 million (25 percent of total search engine requests)[3]

Sexual Sin Is Particularly Damaging

As I talk to spiritual leaders in churches, at national conventions, over the phone, and even in confidential counseling, perhaps the biggest concern we have is the whole realm of sexuality. Even the shepherds—especially the wounded shepherds (and there are *many*)—are falling prey to the seduction of pornography and sexual temptation.

Thanks in part to the private home-delivery system of the Internet, many of the spiritual leaders in America's churches are trying to fill the voids in their hearts with treats and false cures from the world.

Leadership Journal discovered in a survey that 40 percent of evangelical pastors admitted to looking at Internet pornography.[4]

Revered institutions, entire nations, and lofty high courts around the world are seemingly falling in line with the trend toward calling evil *good* and good *evil.*

Recently, as I was writing this book, the supreme court in a certain country voted seven-to-two to approve "group sex" associations, or so-called swinger's clubs, as fully legal. The majority of judges determined, in their highly educated collective opinion, that such deviant sexual activities supposedly "are not detrimental to society."[5] (I can't help but wonder if Rome felt the same way—just before its mighty empire descended into mostly self-induced oblivion.)

Many of the most eager investors for this "growth industry" in this Western nation are from the United States. Those who join for a small amount each month are entitled to full membership "privileges" of having group sex the way they like it. (Paid dues or not, what they call *membership privileges* with the esteemed court's protection, God calls *sin*—and *no* earthly court can rescind or amend His decrees.)

As you may already know, the apostle Paul made it clear there is something about sexual sin that makes it different and somehow more destructive than other sins. Although *all* sin requires the power of God in Christ to be removed, some sins damage more people more thoroughly than others. Paul said:

> Don't you realize that your bodies are actually parts of Christ? Should a man take his body, which belongs to Christ, and join it to a prostitute? Never! And don't you know that if a man joins himself to a prostitute, he becomes one body with her? For the Scriptures say, "The two are united into one." But the person who is joined to the Lord becomes one spirit with him.
>
> Run away from sexual sin! No other sin so clearly affects the body as this one does. For sexual immorality is a sin against your own body. Or don't you know that your body is the temple of the Holy Spirit, who lives in you and was given to you by God?
>
> (1 Corinthians 6:15–19 NLT)

How Do You Fill Your Soul?

Remember, James 1:8 says, "A double minded man is unstable in all his ways" (KJV). Søren Kierkegaard described double-mindedness as "the essential disease of the human spirit." My nephews would say it this way: "No man can serve two honeys."

As we slip down the steep slope toward loss of heart, we begin to doubt what we previously held to be God-given. It is the garden conversation and serpent temptation all over again.

For example, if you felt you were called to ministry—even if you have served faithfully for twenty years—but were brought to your knees through assault or attack, desperation now leads you to think, *Well . . . maybe the ministry is not where I'm supposed to be. Things sure haven't gone very well—in fact, they seem to be going to hell in a handbasket right now. Maybe I need to look in another direction and try something new.* These are the conversations we hear and participate in once we enter the dark gate of adulteries of the heart.

Who but God knows how many people tolerate unspeakable abuses, pain, and brokenness behind the closed doors or America's homes? If even a percentage of these wounded people slip into adulteries of the heart, then hell will be rejoicing for the next ten generations. May hell *not* rejoice on our watch!

Empty and exhausted in our losing struggle, we still reach, hoping and expecting to find something *more* that may finally heal the hurt. Sadly, the more we reach for something that is apart from God, the farther we are from finding the satisfaction we so seek. Solomon was the world's wisest man, but he became lost in his search for pleasure outside of obedience to God when his seven hundred wives and three hundred concubines turned his heart away from God (1 Kings 11:3–12). In the end, as we've seen in previous chapters, he was reduced to a cynical sage of sorrow and doubt.

We Get Tranquilized by the Trivial

According to Ernest Becker, "Modern man is drinking and drugging himself out of awareness or he is shopping, which is the same thing."[6] We get tranquilized by the trivial. There is a growing appetite for adulteries of the heart as more and more people run from their Maker and seek other sources to fill the voids of their souls with activities of the flesh.

There are two times when we are most tempted to turn aside from God to fill our void: when things are going incredibly right (that is another book), and when our lives are collapsing around our ears. This is when we give our attention, our allegiance, and our lives to a substitute for the Real Thing.

We're dabbling with other "lovers," and the "dating" has begun. Once the line has been crossed, a long-term relationship with our lesser lovers is almost impossible. The seeds we've sown from our divided hearts are about to bring an unwelcome and unwholesome harvest. Our adulteries of the heart have set us up for *addiction*.

Abuse is sometime use; addiction is compulsive use and leads to uncontrollable abuse.

Evil flourishes in our pain, wanting us to believe God is not there for us—but He is.

Questions for Discussion and Reflection

1. How do you medicate your emotional pain? When angry, anxious, alone, and alienated, where do you turn— what calms you and seemingly helps to release the pain in your life: Food? Pornography? Work? Drugs? A lover? Excessive shopping?

2. Have you ever just wept in your brokenness? Have you suffered during a season of life that led you into adulteries of the heart? What did it take to awaken you to your idolatries?

3. Do you feel guilt and shame over adulteries of the heart? Is your heart filled with discontent? Can you understand how this can be a good place? Is God trying to get your attention? What would be different if you turned to God in your brokenness?

4. Do you believe that God can rescue you from the adulteries of the heart that hold you in bondage? Will you let Him?

Action Point: Identify any adulteries of the heart you have relied on recently. Determine, one at a time, to defeat them. Replace each with a healthy habit: a daily walk, reading a psalm every day, deepening your relationship with God and others. Stop the spiral while you still can.

· 8 ·

ADDICTION: EMBRACING
THE GODS OF DISTRACTION
Wrapped in Bondage
with the Stench of Hell

It's never enough. What started out as just a few extra hours at the office is now all-consuming. What used to be "a few peeps" at forbidden images online are now consuming hours of irreplaceable time at work and home.

As our pain increases and our confidence in God decreases, the new part-time lovers or distractions we've added to our lives begin to demand more than one night a week in the backseat of our affections.

The void in your life will only grow stronger, and the demands for more time, attention, and commitment can become deafening. It doesn't matter whether the "lover" is flesh and blood, substance abuse, or one of the countless sins of the mind and soul. Maybe you are the only one right now who knows the deeply rooted habit that is taking control. But it always begins to show (see James 1:14–15).

Adulteries of the heart *program us* for addiction, and evil is always ready to collect the debt. With God seemingly out of the picture, the seeds from your divided heart now seek to divide your life among themselves. Your journey now looks like this:

Losing Heart: The Descent into Pain
Ambushed and Assaulted
Anger
Anxiety
Aloneness
Alienation
Arrogance
Adulteries of the Heart
Addiction

As we noted in the last chapter, abuse is sometime use; addiction is compulsive use leading to uncontrollable abuse. As evil flourishes in your pain, the whispers grow louder and more persistent, telling you in countless ways every waking moment: "You have taken on the look, the smell, and the life of hell itself!" Soon the lie progresses. "God *couldn't* love you—just look at you. He's just not there for you."

This produces the key characteristics of addiction in your life: a sense of powerlessness and of numbness. One writer maintained, "Addiction is the most powerful psychic enemy of man's desire for God."[1]

Why? The answer is found in that inverted triangle—anything you pull up into your life to calm or soothe the brokenness may potentially be made into an *idol*, an object of your worship and devotion *other* than God.

Idols may be made of stone, wood, clay, cloth, or the vain imaginations of the mind. Misplaced affections for our children, our ministries, or our pet poodles may all become substitutions for God's presence in our lives. Idols become small gods in the eyes of their beholders.

These small gods don't have to be grand or overtly evil to do damage in our lives. You don't have to kneel down or give offerings to a thing, a person, an activity, or an obsession to make them idols. And these things or people do *not* have to be "evil" to qualify.

✦ *To qualify as an idol, something or someone must simply become a* distraction *from God and His ways.*

In fact, the better and more virtuous a thing is, the greater the potential it has to become an alternative to God. That includes good deeds, religious service, extreme devotion to children or jobs, or even the blind pursuit of a hobby! To qualify as an idol, something or someone must simply become a *distraction* from God and His ways.

Examine everything in your life that suddenly takes on huge meaning and begins to give you purpose, meaning, and value. If God isn't at its core and intimately involved in its pursuit, then you may be playing the lead in a tragedy. You are embracing the gods of distraction, and your newfound "loves" will never satisfy you.

Dallas Willard said, "Social and political revolutions have never been able to transform the heart of darkness that lies deep in the breast of every human being."[2] Only God possesses the cure for what ails us.

Wounded people on a "Jonah path" away from God's presence will board any "ship" promising a rapid journey in the opposite direction. And the world outside of God's kingdom is always ready to supply an endless list of alternative lovers.

It doesn't matter how far we go or how hard we search for purpose and meaning on the journey: whether we participate in escapism through drugs, alcoholism, workaholism, or any other false solution, our problem is obviously spiritual, and so must be the cure.

✦ *Our problem is obviously spiritual,*
and so must be the cure.

Once we finally descend to the loss of heart in full-blown addiction, we discover that we are no longer the masters of our newfound relationship with drug abuse, pornography, or gambling. Several or all of the following characteristics may begin to surface in your life or in the life of someone close to you who has entered the addiction stage of the downward spiral.

Core Characteristics of Addiction and Addictive Behavior[3]

An addiction is a dependence on a substance (alcohol, prescription medicine, marijuana, or street drugs) or activity (gambling, shopping).

An addiction is a physical (as in alcohol or most other drugs) or psychological (as in gambling or shopping) compulsion to use a substance or activity in order to cope with everyday life. For example, without alcohol, the alcoholic does not feel normal and cannot function well.

Addiction is a behavior that is habitual and seemingly impossible to control. It leads to activity the addict uses solely to obtain the substance or cover up its use: the housewife hiding bottles all over the house, the drug addict shoplifting to support the habit, the gambler embezzling to pay off debts.

Characterized by the defense mechanism of denial, the addict blames his or her problems on someone else: the boss is too difficult, the spouse isn't affectionate enough, the kids are disobedient, or the friends are too persuasive. The addict refuses to take responsibility.

Drug addiction is the biochemical dependence on a substance—over time the body needs the substance in ever-increasing amounts to stave off the symptoms of withdrawal.

The Character of Addiction

+ *Unmanageability:* For addicts, their dependency on the substance is out of control.
+ *Neurochemical Tolerance:* God designed our bodies to adapt to what we give them. Therefore, addicts experience tolerance—their bodies need increasing amounts of a chemical to produce the same effect.
+ *Progression:* Many addicts begin by simply experimenting: trying out a drug, going to a casino, taking a puff on a cigarette. However, because more of a chemical is needed to achieve an effect, the addict will increase use of a substance in strength or frequency.
+ *Feelings Avoidance:* The addict uses the substance to improve his or her emotional/psychological state—it is a way of avoiding feelings of loneliness, anxiety, anger, sorrow, etc.

✦ *Consequences:* Estrangement from God, the manifestation of habitual sin, health issues, and social and interpersonal problems are all consequences common to addiction.

Now we can't seem to give up the bottle, the needle, the other woman, or the pornography. We don't have them—they have us! That is how much these lesser lovers have come to mean to our wounded souls.

✦ *Once we finally descend to the loss of heart in full-blown addiction, we discover that we are no longer the masters.*

The Disaster That Occurs

One woman presented to me an unbelievable tale of illusion and addiction. She wound up getting pregnant, then reached out to me at the request of her husband to help her deal with the disaster she had created.

By the grace of God the marriage was saved, but then we had to work through the process of dealing with the child conceived outside of the marriage relationship. She wanted her husband to be an influence in the child's life, so I worked to help them develop acceptance and love for the little boy (since *none* of it was the child's fault).

At the beginning, this same woman had excitedly announced to me that for the first time she had found somebody "who really loved her." Ironically, she learned later that her lover had gotten another woman pregnant at the same time.

Evidently, she wasn't the only one this "special" man "loved." My point is that in the midst of the addictive relationship, this woman was oblivious to all of this. She was incapable of seeing the lie behind the fantasy.

John the apostle warned believers in the first century, "Whosoever is born of God doth not commit sin; for his seed remaineth in him: and he cannot sin, because he is born of God" (1 John 3:9 KJV). That means that if you know Christ, then you can't stay in a sin very long. It is a scary place to be.

John specifically warned us about addictions long ago in his typically blunt style. He said, "Little children, keep yourself from idols" (1 John 5:21 KJV). Basically, anything that comes between you and God has become an idol in your life.

Satan's Goal Is for You to Completely Lose Heart and Give Up

When an addiction seizes control of your life, the accuser comes in to seal the work with his lies. Satan's goal is for you to completely lose heart and give up. He wants nothing less than your destruction.

He is quick to whisper whatever produces the most guilt and shame or unreasoning anger in your heart: "It doesn't matter—go ahead. Nobody cares about you. It's the only way you'll make it through the day."

If all goes his way, your guilt and shame level will escalate until you find yourself completely vulnerable and prone to even more double-mindedness. It somehow becomes easier to turn to your addictive substance again and again just for a brief moment of relief from the painful thoughts of your life.

In the midst of your downward journey, your soul makes the decisive turn toward that temporary cure for the pain. Then your mind begins to be permeated by the presence of that behavior.

Once you begin to believe God no longer loves you or "can't" love you, you have wrapped your pain in a blanket with the stench of hell. The spirit of addiction will leave you feeling out of control and numb from the heart outward.

If you are in trouble in your life, you *know it*. Perhaps you've prayed for forgiveness and you've asked God to help you. You find yourself asking God to cleanse you over and over again. That is a good place to be. James the apostle tells us about the unpleasant alternative: "But each one is tempted when he is drawn away by his own desires and enticed. Then, when desire has conceived, it gives birth to sin; and sin, when it is full-grown, brings forth death" (James 1:14–15).

✦ *Perhaps you've prayed for forgiveness and*
you've asked God to help you. That is a good place to be.

This is my concern for you if you've found yourself trapped in addictions and are losing heart: if you follow this path to its ultimate conclusion, you will begin to die inside. There is a very real possibility that you won't ever hear the call of God again.

We can be certain that God will call, but if you wall yourself in to avoid your pain, you may lose all sense of direction and never respond to the nudge or pulling of God in your life.

Evil works to delude, destroy, and have dominion over you. This may sound very defeating, but the good news is that in reality, Satan has no power over you. *If you are in Christ, it is possible to break the bondage over your life.* There's a way to freedom!

You need to know that, because when you fall into full-blown addiction, it seems as if you've been moved out of the driver's seat and buckled into the back. It is almost as if your life has taken a road of its own and you are just along for the ride.

You begin to feel overwhelmed and unequipped to deal with your life. Your problems have taken on massive dimensions and power. Like Goliath before the armies of Israel, your problem seems to openly defy your faith and mock your character. It shames and terrifies you.

It can spark panic in your soul. Again and again you return to drink, to drugs, to sexual sin, or even to your excessive hobby. In virtually every case, it causes you to become cowardly. This is the goal of the giant in your life: to disdain, despise, and scorn you. It will scream it at your wounded soul: "You're a nobody! You are useless!"

You can either buy the lie of the malevolent whisperer, or you can do what David did—remind yourself of all the times God has delivered you from the lions and the bears in your life. If you fail to remember and renew your faith in God, then ultimately the present-day Goliath looming in your life just might destroy you.

This explains Paul's lament over good people facing bad situations: "I'm terrified for you right now." (Wouldn't it be wonderful if we could *always* follow David's path to victory and shout in the face of the giants before us, "Hey, you're going down! Don't we serve the God who made heaven and earth?")

Any man or woman who commits adulteries of the heart is looking for God.

✦ *Addiction promises you everything but ultimately robs you of everything.*

"I Hate My Life"

Unfortunately, when someone finds he is unsatisfied and *keeps* knocking on the door of his replacement loves in a hopeless attempt to heal his brokenness, he has crossed the line. He has moved from wounded experimentation in adulteries of the heart into the no-man's-land of addiction. Addiction promises you everything but ultimately robs you of everything.

Before long, what was once just a weekend drinking binge becomes a daily necessity. Many things may temporarily medicate the pain, but nothing outside of God can truly calm or soothe the brokenness in your heart.

One day your passing flirtations with Internet pornography or phone sex will suddenly tighten their grip and totally consume your thoughts—and you will hope nobody knows it but you. Someone does know, and no one ever gets away with it. First of all, *you* know. As for the other One, you already know His name.

I don't know how many times good people have come to me in confidence—doctors, fathers, pastors of large churches, Sunday school teachers, and even mothers—to say: "Do you know how many times I've pleaded with God to help me stop? I feel so guilty and so dirty. I don't want to do it—I don't want to break the hearts of my family or disappoint God, but then I just go right back after I pray. I hate my life."

Please understand that evil seeks to exert dominion over you 24/7. Satan knows he is powerless to steal your salvation or anything else God has given to you, so he will do everything he can to influence and compromise you. Satan gets right down on your level and starts whispering lies to your mind:

You are really sick. What a hypocrite. You have no value. In fact, you look a lot like me—you look like hell, you smell like hell, you act like hell. And why not? God does not love you. He's ashamed of you and you know it!

Go ahead and admit what you're thinking. Drink it, it doesn't matter. Click the mouse—at least you'll have a little bit of pleasure. Dial that number and talk to her—she at least *understands* you.

Forget all of that Christian stuff. It's all over anyway— you've already blown it and you're in too far, so get over it. Haven't you heard? The whole world knows and it's time for you to wise up—you can't redeem that which is broken.

Most people lose all heart right here. They resign themselves to the second-best life, pitch camp, and settle in for a long and chilly winter of the soul. It *is* possible to redeem the broken things in your life, but as one thoughtful writer explained, it is not possible or even reasonable to expect to find total safety in life.

The Christian doctrine of suffering explains, I believe, a very curious fact about the world we live in. The settled happiness and security which we all desire, God withholds from us by the very nature of the world: but joy, pleasure, and merriment He has scattered broadcast. We are never safe, but we have plenty of fun, and some ecstasy. It is not hard to see why. The security we crave would teach us to rest our hearts in this world and oppose [become] an obstacle to our return to God: a few moments of happy love, a landscape, a symphony, a merry meeting with our friends, a bath or a football match, have no such tendency. Our Father refreshes us on the journey with some pleasant inns, but will not encourage us to mistake them for home.[4]

Addicted to Unhappiness and Dedicated to Making Others Unhappy

The sad assumption that God doesn't love us when we fall into addiction often produces bitterness—or more properly—the *root of bitterness* in good people. It is often working at the core of our inward pain.

Dr. James Dobson said, "Some of the most bitter, unhappy people on earth are those who have become estranged from the God they no longer understand or trust."[5]

A pastor described someone in a church he served who may well be the epitome of the discontented man. He was faithful to attend services and avoid the "big" sins, but no one could stand to be around him because of his negative and critical attitudes. It seemed as if he was "addicted to unhappiness and dedicated to making others unhappy."

> By the time I met him he was a cranky old guy, but he started when he was a cranky young guy by all accounts. And he just stayed cranky the whole time.
>
> One of the celebrated moments in our church was the time one of the deacons came up to Hank and asked, "Hank, are you happy?" Hank just stood there for a moment and then, without any change of expression on his face or in the tone of his voice, he said, "Yes." And then the brave deacon said, "Well, tell your face." (He never did as far as we could tell.)[6]

The pastor described Hank as a chronic complainer. He even reported the church to the Occupational Safety and Health Administration because he felt the sound levels were too high during worship services! Hank stayed the same year after year, perfecting his crankiness and alienating everyone around him. He seemed to be incapable of loving others as Christ loved him.

> We *expected* Hank to affirm certain doctrines. We *expected* him to know the Bible to a certain extent. We *expected* Hank to attend church, have a quiet time, avoid certain sins, tithe, and do some church work.
> We did *not* expect to see Christ formed in him day after day, week after week, month after month, and year after year.[7]

This man obviously had a serious heart problem, but the church had problems as well. The pastor's point is that we should expect to see genuine transformation in our lives, not mere religious conformation to rules and guidelines.

Pain Has a Purpose

I should warn you that true transformation usually occurs in the middle of pain and life's adversities. Wouldn't it be better to train Christians to live in hope and faith while they walk together through the rough and difficult passages of life? These journeys through pain are precisely what help us experience transformation into Christ's image day by day!

> ✦ *God often uses the pain we fear the most to save us from our self-made hell on earth!*

Our flight from pain often puts us on the downward path toward the loss of heart. It begins with anger but ends with addiction or idolatry of the heart. It seems odd, but in fact God often uses the pain we fear the most to save us from our self-made hell on earth!

If C. S. Lewis was right, perhaps the first purpose of pain is to shatter the idea that "all is well." God is willing to break through our illusions and shatter our romance with small-time idols—even at the risk of driving us to all-out rebellion.

> No doubt Pain as God's megaphone is a terrible instrument; it may lead to final and unrepented rebellion. But it gives the only opportunity the bad man can have for amendment. It removes the veil; it plants the flag of truth within the fortress of the rebel soul.
>
> If the first and lowest operation of pain shatters the illusion that all is well, the second shatters the illusion that what we have, whether good or bad in itself, is our own and enough for us.[8]

In the end, as good people who finally arrive at the destination of our journey to the loss of heart, we may feel as if we've descended so low that pain seems to be our lot in life. The evil whisperer has almost convinced us that God really isn't there for us.

Yet, there is something inside us, something no evil can turn and no darkness can dim, that refuses to yield. Some still, small voice stands against all of the lies, the failures, the hopelessness, and the pain to whisper truth to our broken hearts: "Oh, but He *is* there. He is there for *you*."

The fact that you and I suffer does not prove God's indifference, weakness, or disappearance. As George MacDonald said, "The Son of God suffered unto the death, not that men might not suffer, but that their sufferings might be like His."[9] And I might add, *that their rewards and resurrection might be like His.*

✦ *The fact that you and I suffer does* not *prove*
God's indifference, weakness, or disappearance.

Divine Discontent

If you are worth anything to God (and you *are*—if you need an objective measure of your worth, consider the price Jesus paid for you on the cross), then a spirit of discontent will erupt inside of you in that journey to brokenness and addiction.

Divine discontent is not a bad thing, it's a good thing!

That's the place where God does His best work. If you're begging for a better day, that means He is alive within your spirit. If your heart's crying out, "It's not the way it's supposed to be!" then there is hope.

One simple decision of the heart determines where you go from here. God is there, God cares, and He still loves you. He has *always* loved you: even on your worst day, doing your worst deed, even as you were shouting your loudest and angriest curse at the heavens, your Father in heaven loved you.

You may not realize it yet, but your path to healing has already begun. Just learning how things can spin into outright chaos and confusion when life isn't the way it is supposed to be can help get you moving past those sticking places in life.

More importantly, you begin to see things differently once you honestly face what has happened in your life, examine the decisions you've made in your pain, and recognize the attempts you've made to recover what was lost. Once you begin to see the *how* of it all, then you are staged to heal.

If your heart can grasp even the slightest part of this truth, if you can see even the slimmest ray of light in your cave of despair . . . there is hope!

Questions for Discussion and Reflection

1. What have become distractions from God and His ways in your life? In other words, what are your idols: Money? Power? Possessions? Extreme religious behavior? Forbidden physical pursuits? New exotic sensations?

2. Examine everything in your life that suddenly takes on huge meaning and begins to give you purpose and value. Is God at the core?

3. Please understand that evil seeks to exert dominion over you 24/7. The mistaken belief that God doesn't love us often produces bitterness. But remember that God often uses the pain we fear the most to save us from our self-made hell on earth! This is the purpose of the cross. Have you believed the lie that God doesn't love you? Why? What Scriptures refute this lie?

Action Point: If your casual adultery of the heart has become a raging addiction, start today to overcome it. Confess it to someone: a pastor, a spiritual mentor, a qualified Christian counselor. No matter what, don't try to face down your addiction alone. God—and those who love Him—are more than ready to help you.

· PART II ·

Recovery of Heart:
Coming Out of Pain

· 9 ·

THE AFFECTION OF THE
PURSUING GOD
A Love That Will Not Let Me Go

Have you ever noticed that once you hit bottom with no options or avenues of escape, it seems you are living in the worst of times and the best of times? How can that be? Perhaps it is because, in one sense, as bad as things may seem, the only way to go is up.

Even in your darkest moment, if Christ dwells in you, there is a song deep in your soul that sings, "He will make a way. Someday, everything's going to change because God will make a way for me."

The mind may forget, but the heart always remembers Him who said, "I am the LORD thy God, which brought thee out of the land of Egypt: open thy mouth wide, and I will fill it" (Ps. 81:10 KJV).

The downward spiral toward the loss of heart can leave us

feeling stranded, abandoned, and in despair—with little desire or ability to help ourselves. Perhaps we've had it all wrong. One writer made clear in his writings that God always has His way: "The first man [Jesus] serves God as a son, and the second [mankind] as a tool. For you will certainly carry out God's purpose, however you act, but it makes a difference to you whether you serve like Judas or like John."[1]

You are in the sights of the Pursuer God. We don't pursue Him as much as He pursues us. That's probably why you're reading this book. He has been gently calling you. What happens next is up to you. What will you do, how will you respond when He reaches out toward you? Will you respond like Judas or like John?

God's supernatural love is the greatest change agent in the human soul! God's love *for you* is literally beyond measure. In the introduction I mentioned the prodigal son who left his father to strike out into the world in pursuit of pleasure. He went from a position of favor and total provision in his father's house to sleeping and eating with the pigs, used up and discarded by his party-time friends once his money was gone.

When he finally woke up from his sin-drugged stupor, he wondered, *Why am I sitting here between this stinking sow and her piglets and fighting with them over the slop in this pen? I could be in my father's house! Maybe he will let me come home. Even if I stay in the servants' quarters, it will be better than this!*

This man's father *was* looking for him. His love never weakened, and his desire to see his son restored only grew with every passing day of separation. As for the prodigal son, the love of his father was still in him. When he finally "came to himself" (Luke 15:17), he quickly made the decision: "I'm going home."

> ✦ *Sometimes we have to eat with the hogs*
> *before we can really appreciate our Father's table.*

We are more like the prodigal son than we care to admit! Sometimes we have to eat with the hogs before we can really appreciate our Father's table. We must exhaust our money and squander our peace in pursuit of lesser lovers before we truly recognize the unconditional nature of our Father's abiding love and understand that there is no life in the things we've chased after.

We Are Not Big Enough to Choose Wisely

Author Philip Yancey said it well in his book, *Where Is God When It Hurts?*

> It is hard to be a creature. We think we are big enough to run our own world without such messy matters as pain and suffering to remind us of our dependence. We think we are wise enough to make our own decisions about morality, to live rightly without the megaphone of pain blaring in our ears. We are wrong, as the Garden of Eden story proves. Man and woman, in a world without suffering, chose against God.
>
> And so we who have come after Adam and Eve have a choice. We can trust God. Or we can blame Him, not ourselves, for the world.[2]

It seems we have to reach the end of ourselves before we finally discover our *true selves* in the healing embrace of the Father's heart.

When my son, Zach, was much younger, he became angry with me over a particular situation, and I picked him up to hold him. He arched his back and struggled to get down, kicking his feet in anger.

I drew him even closer, held him tight, and said, "Dad loves you." Zach just buried his face in my chest and went limp. That was what he wanted all along.

When our children are in trouble or feel upset, where do we want them to go? We want them to come right into our arms. In fact, I can't *wait* until Zach or Megan lands in my arms so we can find forgiveness together. It is a place my children long to be.

We can't effectively deal with our angry or hurt children until they calm down. Once they release the anger, pain, or fear and go limp in our arms, then we can deal with them.

It is when we're touching each other in unconditional love that they relax. They're with Dad then. They know the way I feel about them; they know the price I will pay to keep them secure, happy, and at peace in life. Once they feel safe from the storm, we can begin to talk our way through any problems they're facing.

It is that loving embrace of our heavenly Father that brings peace and restoration. He is the Father to the fatherless.

The Care of God: "It Will Drive the Burden of Sorrow Far from Him"

When you understand the affection of God, it opens the door for you to show others godly affection. Euripides once said, "The care of God is a great thing to our soul. If a man believes it in his heart, it will drive the burden of sorrow far from him."

The most important thing to understand in all of this is that your Father is always there. You and I have always had an audience of one. Our heavenly Father's love burns just as brightly for us whether we are walking out of a church service or crawling out of a seedy bar.[3]

Our journey now looks like this:

Losing Heart: The Descent into Pain
Ambushed and Assaulted
Anger
Anxiety
Aloneness
Alienation
Arrogance
Adulteries of the Heart
Addiction
Recovery of Heart: Coming Out of Pain
Affection of God

✦ *Our heavenly Father's love burns just as brightly for us whether we are walking out of a church service or crawling out of a seedy bar.*

Think about it. Has God been whispering your name? Has somebody been talking to you in spite of your porcupine demeanor? Has someone been trying to reach you—even though you haven't taken phone calls for a month? How many people have said something kind to you, even in the face of your unkindness toward them? In fact, who gave you this book? And why did you decide to read it?

Something is going on; something good is happening right in the middle of your bad dream. The truth is *still* true, even if you stepped away from the table for a while. Jesus said, "No man can come to me, except the Father which hath sent me draw him" (John 6:44 KJV). Paul wrote, "For God is working in you, giving you the *desire* to obey him and the *power* to do what pleases him" (Phil. 2:13 NLT, emphasis mine).

Right in the middle of your worst living nightmare, at your most un-Christian moment, God is at work. Many times we actually begin to think we get out of our messes by pursuing God. There *is* a time when we seek Him, but the deeper truth is that anything good that happens occurs only because of *Him*. It isn't you pursuing God, it's the other way around.

Our Father in heaven is the Pursuer God. He understands our feelings of brokenness, and He loves to use powerlessness to send us fleeing back to His arms. He is waiting.

If you feel a nagging state of discontent in your life, if something inside you *knows* that your life is not the way it's supposed to be; if you even imagine the words, *I've got to do something different, God has been speaking*. That isn't you. He literally is chasing after you. Os Guiness said:

> That discontent, that stab in your heart, is simply the cry of your heart that all is not right. Surely there is something more. . . .
>
> Made for relationship, in brokenness the heart yearns for something more. . . .
>
> You may not believe it right now but God loves you. He has been softly and tenderly whispering your name. He has never given up on you and even now yearns for your heart. He wants to wash you clean and to help you start all over again. And you can. It doesn't matter what you've done or where you've been. It's all about who He is and what He has done that matters.[4]

God has been reaching out to you, and He is waiting. If you want to be free, don't stop here. It doesn't matter whether you are a factory worker, secretary, corporate president, or pastor of a megachurch. You are not alone. All around you, people are hurting and searching for what only God can give.

I can't tell you how many pastors I've met who have asked, "Do you think God still wants me? Do you think He still wants to use me? Tim, I want Him to forgive me and wash me clean. I want Him to put that message in my heart that I love. Somewhere I just got lost. And nobody's talked to me, nobody." True freedom comes when you surrender to God at the point of your greatest weakness. "It was for freedom that Christ set us free" (Gal. 5:1 NASB). We want that release to freedom more than anything because that is what we were made for.

"Daddy, Catch Me!"

After struggling with our insecurity and instability for so long, when we finally let go we feel lighter than air. We are once again five-year-olds waiting with anticipation to leap off the steps into open arms with a joyful shout and loud laughter, saying, "Daddy, catch me!"

Something beautiful happens in your soul when you finally *believe* that God's heart is toward you—no matter what. He is the Dad who doesn't want you to go anywhere else but into His arms. He is saying, "Come to Me. I am not going to fail you. I want to show you a way to a better life." He's been waiting for you.

My thoughts often turn to my mother, who is now with the Lord. My mother believed in me. She always thought I could climb any mountain in existence. She was "good people." Her unconditional love and support for me taught me a great deal about how God feels toward us: "It doesn't matter where you've been, it doesn't matter what you've done: you are my child."

I've learned to hear God whispering, "Do you know what, Tim? I forgive you. Get up. Get back on track. Now let's go."

It is out of a heart of affection that God begins to set your heart free. That is why it is so important that you and I understand that God really loves us, and His love is unconditional.

One of the marks of a good counselor is his or her willingness to say, "I'm going to stay with you until we're done. We'll see this through together. I'm committed. I will love unceasingly and be there, come hell or high water." I want to see hurting people made whole. I want to see fractured lives put back together through the power of Jesus Christ. Helping people through this process is what I was born to do.

A lady called as I was working on this book to say, "I appreciate your taking care of that hard situation for me." I thought, *That's just what I'm supposed to do. It isn't me.* If we don't have time to help each other, what in the world are we doing here?

God Is Not Proud— He Stoops to Conquer

For reasons we will fully understand only in God's presence, our Creator loves us so much that He will disregard His own pride and perfection to reach out to us. C. S. Lewis wrote:

> It is a poor thing to strike our colours [surrender the ship] to God when the ship is going down under us; a poor thing to come to Him as a last resort, to offer up "our own" when it is no longer worth keeping. If God were proud He would hardly have us on such terms: but He is not proud, He

stoops to conquer, He will have us even though we have shown that we prefer everything else to Him, and come to Him because there is "nothing better" now to be had. The same humility is shown by all those Divine appeals to our fears which trouble high-minded readers of scripture. It is hardly complimentary to God that we should choose Him as an alternative to Hell: yet even this He accepts. The creature's illusion of self-sufficiency must, for the creature's sake, be shattered; and by trouble or fear of trouble on earth, by crude fear of the eternal flames, God shatters it "unmindful of His glory's diminution."[5]

This is our Pursuer God in action. He will follow us in our rebellion, pursue us in our pain, and humble us on the mountaintop. He loves us that much.

Ironically, one of the greatest places of spiritual assault is in our success. God's complaint against the Israelites in Deuteronomy 31:20 was that when they "are satisfied and become prosperous, then they will turn to other gods and serve them, and spurn Me" (NASB).

One of the most beautiful things about God's love is that He constantly speaks to us—even in our pain. It is possible to get beyond the cacophony of the crazy noise that surrounds you. Once you do, you will hear the gentle whisper of God.

✦ *This is a divine moment.*
He is calling you to a new life.

This much I know: He wants you to be free. He wants you to start on a new journey. This is a divine moment. He is calling you to a new life. He's whispering your name.

Hell mutters in cynical scorn, "Don't bother. You're too far gone, your life is wasted, and you didn't have that much to offer anyway. You just don't matter anymore—all of that junk you hear is just another cruel joke. Don't you get it? *Nobody* cares."

Your Father in heaven sings a different tune—an *eternal* one: "Come on home, My daughter. I've been waiting for you, son. You don't know how much I've wept over you, preserved you, and moved people, resources, and divine opportunities into your life. I'm here. I've *always* been here, and I will never leave you."

That is the heart of Jesus. "Jerusalem, Jerusalem . . . How often I wanted to gather your children together, the way a hen gathers her chicks under her wings, and you were unwilling" (Matt. 23:37 NASB). You were made for God and you'll never find happiness—that divine discontent will never go away—until you reconnect with the One who made you. He loves you, He knows your pain, He hears your cry. "The LORD is near to the brokenhearted / And saves those who are crushed in spirit" (Ps. 34:18 NASB).

C. S. Lewis said, "God whispers to us in our pleasures, speaks to us in our conscience, but shouts to us in our pain. Pain is God's megaphone to rouse a deaf world."[6]

God Still Opens Deaf Ears and Blind Eyes— and Sometimes He Uses Pain

Sometimes it takes the pain of loss, assault, alienation, arrogance, adulteries of the heart, and even addiction to open our deaf ears and bring light to our blind eyes.

One minister wrote, "I was recently involved in a survey in which hundreds of people were asked to identify the factors that were most formative in their spiritual growth. The number one response overwhelmingly involved times of suffering and pain."[7]

Unless pain is part of our personal journey, we have little help to offer people who are suffering pain.

✦ *Unless pain is part of our personal journey,*
we have little help to offer people who are suffering pain.

Gloria Gaither, the prolific songwriter, wife, and singing partner with Bill Gaither, asked 250 writers and publishers at a Gospel Music Association workshop, "How many of you are involved in praise and worship?" When nearly everyone raised a hand, she asked a second question: "How many of you, who obviously spend your life in praise and worship, have read 1 and 2 Kings in the last two years?" When only three hands went up, she leaned forward and said:

> Then what right have you to go through the Psalms to pick out a few positive lines here and there? Because most of the Psalms is beating the chest and lament and "I don't know if God exists" and "I don't know where He went" and "I don't know if He loves me." Finally the psalmist resolves a few things—and we'll find one little line and have it on the screen by Sunday morning. But what right have you to take his line that he paid for if you don't know what he paid to get it there?[8]

God *will* see you through this valley of yours if you will allow Him to. And when you come through, you will have something powerful to say about God's love and faithfulness—because you have paid for it in the valley by yielding to Him (one way or another).

Once you know that God really loves you, it is as if you've

finally found the fuse box in the basement. Once power is restored, light expels the darkness in every room of your house. Problems come into proper focus and find their solution in Him.

He is the key to your life, your future, and your happiness. There is no other, for every other good thing, every wonderful person, and every fulfilling purpose comes from Him.

Life becomes a great adventure when you return to your Father's arms. Your challenges may still be there, but the burdens seem to drop away in His strong embrace.

Deuteronomy 33:27 says, "The eternal God is your refuge, / And underneath are the everlasting arms." In other words, no matter how low you go, His arms are still ready to bear you up. Now *that* is how you come out of pain!

You Are About to Discover God at His Best

Perhaps you feel you've hit rock bottom in your life. No one else may know, and you feel you can't even talk about it with anyone else. You may be struggling with financial pain, sinful addictions, and brokenness all at once! You may have hundreds or thousands of people looking to you for leadership in the church, and you are desperately wondering in your private pain, "God, are You there?"

Are you living a false life, hiding behind a façade of false strength and confidence? Do you live in fear that it will take only one more thing to shatter your life? Peter the apostle understood the pain of failure and betrayal. He said, "Beloved, do not think it strange concerning the fiery trial which is to try you, as though some strange thing happened to you" (1 Pet. 4:12).

I have great news for you! It is exactly when the thunder is the loudest and the storm gales seem the strongest—it is when your burdens seem too heavy to bear that God is at His best! No sorrow leaves you where it found you. You are going to get bitter or you are going to get better. When you've moved into the state of addiction, you are very near the end of the journey to loss of heart. The only thing left—other than the total loss of heart and life—is to turn around, leave bitterness behind, run to your Father's outstretched arms, and find His dream for your life.

✦ *No sorrow leaves you where it found you.*

Release your hurts, stop focusing on what is lost, and concentrate on what is left. Don't swallow the hurt, don't rehearse the hurt, and don't seek revenge. It is time to return to the "God of all comfort" and surrender to His love (2 Cor. 1:3).

Life always moves forward. Don't expect things to go back to normal. They won't. You have the opportunity to create a new normal, a new and better life—but you can't do it alone.

The Affection of God Takes Him Places We Don't Expect Him to Go

The affection of God is really the *pursuit of God:* this is God in action, the God who is always with you. In fact, it is His affection that takes Him places we just don't expect Him to go— He goes *everywhere* you go. Perhaps He is the silent person who sat beside you at every bar stool you visited last year.

One man struggled with God as he lost his battle with

alcoholism. He wound up in a bar night after night, and it was really breaking the heart of one of his daughters. She wept for her dad day after day. One night when he didn't come home yet again, she thought, *I'll just go find him.*

She found the bar and walked up behind him. He was slumped over and half-drunk when she tapped his right shoulder and said, "Daddy, I want you to come home."

When he turned and saw the face of his little girl, he just put his head down and cried. God was shouting to him through his little girl!

It is decision time for all of us who have allowed pain to drive us to addiction. It is time to change things: we need a radical transformation.

The good news is that through this incident, this man was finally able to face his problem, surrender to God, and get help. When he came to me, he sealed his decision with the words, "I'm done, Tim." He made the turn and took the first real step on his journey *back* to the recovery of heart. He was coming out of his pain.

✦ *Once you discover He loves you,*
nothing can hold you back!

God is right there in *your* pain too. He is even there beside you in your success. He already knows your fears, your frailties, and your future.

Without the affection of God there is nothing for you, but once you discover He loves you, nothing can hold you back! His love literally empowers you in your powerlessness to send you fleeing back to Him.

It doesn't matter where you've been or what you've done. If you turn your back to the battle to answer His voice, you will realize that nothing has disqualified you from the love of God in Christ. He weeps over you as your loving heavenly Father, and through His love He works even through your pain.

Joni Eareckson Tada is a remarkable woman, author, artist, and Christian speaker today. But she had to persevere despite a catastrophic spinal injury that left her a quadriplegic as a young woman. She taught me a valuable principle a few years ago when I asked her what it was like for her to wake up each morning and deal with her formidable challenges.

---

*   *I've learned that His presence is enough.*

Joni said, "Tim, it's just awful." I was interviewing her for the radio program and she told me she was having a bad day. I knew she had been crying.

She said, "Tim, I'm feeling terrible, but I've really gotten to a place where I've learned that His presence is enough. That's all I need. So when I understand that," she said, "I say, 'Face, put on a smile.' Then," she said, "I smile. And then I try to face another day."[9]

God is able to work through *everything* in your life—the good, the bad, the beautiful, and the ugly. God works in *everything* to win your heart. According to Philip Yancey, "He will never do anything to destroy the need for faith. In fact, He guides us through times of testing specifically to cultivate that belief and dependence on Him (Hebrews 11:6–7)."[10]

My friend Dr. Gary Sibcy pointed out something simple but profound while teaching on the passage in Philippians 4 that describes what we should focus on for a healthy and godly thought life. He pointed everyone back to one simple sentence in Philippians 4:5 that says, "The Lord is near" (NIV). And that is why we must "be anxious for nothing, but in everything by prayer and supplication with thanksgiving let your requests be made known to God" (Phil. 4:6 NASB).

Before we move one page beyond this chapter, this verse must be a living reality in our hearts and thinking. If we can't or won't believe and stand on this promise from God, then we must retrace our steps until we can and will: " 'For I know the plans that I have for you,' declares the LORD, 'plans for welfare and not for calamity to give you a future and a hope' " (Jer. 29:11 NASB).

The affection of God for us does what nothing else can do: it breaks through the prison walls of deception that evil has woven in our lives. It silences the whispered half-truths and endless jabs from "the accuser of our brethren." Once the affection of God pierces the darkness of the soul, light begins to transform your perceptions and rekindle hope.

> And I heard a loud voice saying in heaven, Now is come salvation, and strength, and the kingdom of our God, and the power of his Christ: for the accuser of our brethren is cast down, which accused them before our God day and night.
> (Revelation 12:10 KJV)

Questions for Discussion and Reflection

1. Think about it. Has God been whispering your name? Has somebody been talking to you in spite of your demeanor? Has someone been trying to dial your number—even though you haven't taken phone calls for a month? How many people have said something kind to you, even in the face of your unkindness toward them? In fact, who gave you this book? And why did you decide to read it?

2. Have you ever come to the "end of yourself"? How did you know you needed to change? Where did new experiences of affection for God come from?

3. Have you ever thought it just may be that *your Father* is pursuing *you?* That it really is Him, and that it is *all about Him?*

4. How has God used pain in your life to bring you back to Him?

Action Point: How can you respond to God's pursuit of you? Can you begin to reach out to Him, both by yourself and with others? Make a list of the ways God touches your life every day with His goodness, and thank Him. Look for things — no matter how small — that you can do for Him.

· 10 ·

EXPOSED TO LOVE
AND ASSESSING OUR MESS
Gazing at Perfection and
Pinpointing Our Imperfection

The more you understand God's deep affection for you, the more you see your utmost need of Him and want to please Him. When you see or experience the best, you reevaluate the rest. It is almost a reflex.

When you pull into an auto dealership in your 1979 mini-van, freshly washed and vacuumed though it may be, something happens when you step onto the showroom floor. Perhaps it is the shiny paint, the smell of the new tires, leather upholstery, and all of the gadgets you've never had before. Maybe you're amazed to see sliding car doors that don't fall off.

Whatever it is, whether or not you choose to buy what you saw inside, another thing happens outside. You begin to assess and compare what you have with what you could have. Your journey now looks like this:

Losing Heart: The Descent into Pain
Ambushed and Assaulted
Anger
Anxiety
Aloneness
Alienation
Arrogance
Adulteries of the Heart
Recovery of Heart: Coming Out of Pain
Affection of God
Assessment

When it is your *life* parked outside, and the showroom is the throne room of God, then the value of even the briefest exposure to His glory and love is immeasurable!

It happened to Isaiah the prophet. He walked into the temple just as he had countless times before. Perhaps he was satisfied with the way things were going—he had already delivered about five chapters' worth of prophecies to God's people. Isaiah was the head man when it came to hearing and proclaiming God's will in those days. It is also possible that he was still dealing with grief over King Uzziah's death. In any case, the day came when everything changed.

> In the year King Uzziah died, I saw the Lord sitting on a throne, high and lifted up, and the train of His robe filled the temple. Above it stood seraphim; each one had six wings: with two he covered his face, with two he covered his feet, and with two he flew. And one cried to another and said,

"Holy, holy, holy is the LORD of hosts;
the whole earth is full of His glory!"

And the posts of the door were shaken by the voice of him
who cried out, and the house was filled with smoke.

(Isaiah 6:1–4)

What a sight! What would happen to *you* if you walked into
your local church building, bulletin in hand, and looked up to
see this?

Isaiah Saw Perfection and Confessed His Imperfection

I suspect you might do the same thing Isaiah did. When he saw
the Lord in all of His glory and perfection, he immediately
started to confess what he saw about himself—his imperfec-
tions.

So I said,

"Woe is me, for I am undone! ["My destruction is
sealed"—NLT]
Because I am a man of unclean lips,
And I dwell in the midst of a people of unclean lips;
For my eyes have seen the King,
The LORD of hosts."

(Isaiah 6:5)

Why did Isaiah act this way? He found himself in the presence of someone who was truly holy, high and lifted up. His
very next thought turned to how sinful his life looked in comparison!

This is the beginning of the assessment process. When God is involved, assessment is entirely healthy and necessary. (In the case of an encounter with a shiny new vehicle on a showroom floor, it might not be entirely necessary *or* healthy for your pocketbook.)

To a lesser extent, the same process happens when the Holy Spirit illuminates God's Word as we read it, hear it proclaimed, or meditate on it. It should spark a godly comparison between the life you're living and the life God has anointed you to live.

Charles H. Spurgeon wrote, "Those who navigate little streams and shallow creeks, know but little of the God of the tempests; but those who 'do business in great waters,' these see His 'wonders in the deep.' Among the huge Atlantic waves of bereavement, poverty, temptation, and reproach, we learn the power of Jehovah, because we feel the littleness of man."

God's Cure for "Identity Forgetfulness"

Many of us landed in our dark time due to a condition the Bible describes. It is a kind of "identity forgetfulness" that occurs when we *hear* God's Word but fail to *do* it: "For if anyone is a hearer of the word and not a doer, he is like a man observing his natural face in a mirror; for he observes himself, goes away, and immediately forgets what kind of man he was. But he who looks into the perfect law of liberty and continues in it, and is not a forgetful hearer but a doer of the work, this one will be blessed in what he does" (James 1:23–25).

Think about how many people you know who work really hard to prove that they are okay. It is as if they don't have any self-awareness—they don't know who they are anymore. In most cases, they simply see themselves in their pain. They remind me of a married couple trying to navigate the rapids of life when they are both looking through thick eyeglasses of pain.

The husband believes that everything his wife does is calculated to hurt him. For her part, she is responding blindly out of her brokenness. She is dying on the inside, so her whole life is a response to pain. The husband just happens to be the one in the way most of the time.

✦ *They don't see how accepted and how loved they are.*

When I work with my clients, I see their wounded places; I search for sore points indicating hidden bruises or soul wounds. Pain so clouds their vision that they have little or no understanding of God's love. They don't see how accepted and how loved they are—they are unaware that God the great Pursuer is hot on the "heels" of their hearts.

When He finally captures our attention through His affection, we are undone. When we feel His healing touch pierce our pain, it dawns on us: *He is here, He is faithful, and He loves me. Because He's here, I can be set free! But oh, just look at me!*

We are like people who have come out of a yearlong coma: we look like wrecks and we're a bit dazed. This is where God steps in through His mercy and grace to do for us what we cannot do for ourselves—as He did for Isaiah.

> Then one of the seraphim flew to me, having in his hand a live coal which he had taken with the tongs from the altar. And he touched my mouth with it, and said,
>
> > "Behold, this has touched your lips;
> > Your iniquity is taken away,
> > And your sin purged."
>
> (Isaiah 6:6–7)

What Started You on the Descent of Pain?

Do you remember the account of Jesus at the pool of Bethesda? He asked a crippled man, "Do you want to be made well?" (John 5:6). Healing is a choice, and new life starts with a taste of the affection of God and the quest to understand what has happened in your life. What started you on the descent of pain to the loss of heart? It's time for a vital, eye-opening assessment of the behaviors in your life that you need to purge.

David, the king and psalmist, the one God said was "a man after His own heart" (1 Sam. 13:14), underwent many heart-wrenching assessments of his life. We can borrow his prayer in confidence because it is a prayer God is quick to answer: "Search me, O God, and know my heart: try me, and know my thoughts: and see if there is any wicked way in me, and lead me in the way everlasting" (Ps. 139:23–24 KJV).

In many ways, this part of your journey matches what a soldier does before a battle: he checks his gear for weaknesses, breaks, and missing pieces. He sharpens his bayonet, restocks his ammunition, and tests his communication equipment.

This is an appropriate analogy, as Dr. Dan Allender points out in *The Healing Path*. As God helps us back on our feet and onto the road of recovery, we may realize that we are in a battle: "God had been deepening my conviction that every moment of life is warfare, a battle against evil's hatred of *glory*. And every battle is won or lost to the degree our heart is open to the pleasure God has crafted for us to enter, embrace, and enjoy."[1]

Are the Shelves Stocked, or Is My Heart Lean and Bare?

Part of your life assessment includes asking these questions: *What sinful behaviors in my life do I need to purge? What good attributes are missing or in low supply? Do I have a rich supply of the things Paul said should be there: love, joy, peace, long-suffering, kindness, goodness, faithfulness, gentleness, self-control. Are the shelves stocked, or is my heart lean and bare?*

These are just simple things, nothing grand. They are outward proof of His inward presence and power in your life. As you let them remind you of the love of God, courage and self-acceptance will begin to flow back into your life and transform even ordinary things you do each day.

It has been said that "God never wastes a wound." I believe that is true, but I've noticed we often *can* and *do* waste our moments and squander our wounds! We discover great wisdom the day we begin to learn from our mistakes and sins and avoid going through the pain of them all over again.

✦ *No soul that seriously and constantly desires joy will ever miss it.*

Paul said, "I can do all things through Christ who strengthens me" (Phil. 4:13). God will see you through as long as you choose His way. C. S. Lewis put everything into perspective when he wrote: "There are only two kinds of people in the end: those who say to God, 'Thy will be done,' and those to whom God says, '*Thy* will be done.' All that are in Hell, choose it. Without that self-choice there could be no Hell. No soul that seriously and constantly desires joy will ever miss it. Those who seek find. To those who knock, it is opened."[2]

You are here, making assessments of your life, precisely because you *have* made some right choices. You may feel as if you are at the bottom of a deep ravine, but you dared to say to the God who pursues, "*Thy* will be done." He pursued you and has awakened you. Now He has shown you the door that leads you up and out. It's time to knock on the door of opportunity.

The Assessment Continues

Perhaps the most important part of your life to examine for damaging habits is your relationships. The Word of God tells us to avoid being tossed back and forth by the waves of words in life: "We should no longer be children, tossed to and fro and carried about with every wind of doctrine, by the trickery of men, in the cunning craftiness of deceitful plotting, but, speaking the truth in love, may grow up in all things into Him who is the head—Christ" (Eph. 4:14–15).

The assessment process provides a damage report that shows how we have harmed our vital relationships, and how we may repair those problems and avoid them in the future.

✦ *The assessment process provides a damage report*
that shows how we have harmed our vital relationships.

Many of our most destructive patterns show up in the way we communicate with other people. This excerpt from my book cowritten with Dr. Gary Sibcy, *Why You Do the Things You Do*, sheds some light on these patterns:

John Gottman, renowned scientist and family psychologist, found four kinds of unhealthy communication that interfere with our ability to resolve negative feelings following an attachment injury. He calls these the "Four Horsemen to the Apocalypse" (in other words, a ride toward the end):

Criticism. To explain what we mean by *criticism*, we'll compare it to a *complaint*. Complaints are generally specific: "I don't like it when you tell me you're going to take out the trash and you don't do it." Criticism, however, is much more global and is sometimes packaged as a question that implies the other person has a character flaw: "Why do you always do that? You never do what you say you're going to do. This is just another example of how I can't count on you for anything."

Defensiveness. When we receive criticism, it's easy to retaliate with countercriticism: "What do you mean I never do what I say? What about the dishes? When's the last time they were piled up all over the counter? Is that all you can do, whine and complain? No wonder you can't get anyone to do anything for you!" Countercriticism and an "I'm-a-victim, why-does-everything-have-to-happen-to-me" attitude are both forms of defensiveness.

Contempt. When criticism and defensiveness are ratcheted up several notches, they can lead to derogatory remarks, put-downs, and extreme disrespect. For example, not mowing the grass can lead to "You make me sick! You never do what you say you'll do. You're a big talker, just like your mother, but you never follow through. I've grown used to not being able to rely on you, so I'll just do everything myself, like always."

Stonewalling. When the intensity gets too strong, a person can shut down and decide he or she will no longer participate in the conversation. The person may walk out of the room or just stop talking and stare off into space. One of our clients called this the thousand-yard stare. In the heat of the argument, it would, understandably, drive his wife crazy, intensifying her rage and setting up the battle for another round of criticism.[3]

Dr. Gottman's research focused on marriage or family relationships, but it applies to almost any relationship. Gary and I also noted that "what seems to distinguish healthy from unhealthy couples is their ability to repair the damage done."[4]

This is especially appropriate as we assess our lives. We want to see what has happened, what is wrong, and how we can correct these things God's way. It is the only way we can move forward to recover our hearts and come out of the pain.

✦ *When you saw God's love for you, you began to see yourself more clearly.*

Our Role Model

The best thing that could happen already has. When you saw God's love for you, you began to see yourself more clearly. God's fatherly affection for you—with its purity, beauty, and unimaginable strength—sets you up to honestly assess your life because it is simply the natural thing to do. Socrates said, "The unexamined life is not worth living." He was right.

Accurate assessment, or what the Bible calls "a sober measure" of yourself (see Rom. 12:3), is one of your best safeguards against what one psychologist calls "pseudo-transformation." (Another word for this is *hypocrisy*.)

There is no miracle like the miracle of a changed life.

The thing that gripped you somewhere along the line gripped me too—[the idea] that I could be used somehow by God to be part of a changed life. To see a heart that was wounded or bitter or cold become loving. To see a spirit that was in despair receive hope and joy.

I think that's why you're here. But I think when people don't experience that, sometimes they give up. That's one bad thing that happens when people don't experience authentic transformation.

The second one, I think, is even worse. I think for many people, when they don't experience authentic transformation, they settle for what might be called pseudo-transformation.[5]

How do you assess something? You must have a measure, an ideal, an icon of perfection, a prototype that portrays the original intent of the designer. Does this sound vaguely familiar?

Jesus Christ is Author and Finisher of our faith. He is the Last Adam, the Alpha and Omega—the Beginning and the End. He is the Firstborn of many sons. In Him was the fullness of the godhead bodily.

Isaiah saw Him in the temple and it totally transformed his life and ministry.

You and I met Him heart to heart, and Immanuel literally came to dwell in us. We bear God's indelible portrait of Himself in our hearts and we see His ideal servant portrayed in detail in the Word of God.

It is from this prototype Son, the first of many sons and daughters, that we draw all dimensions and guidelines for the way a Christian—a Christlike person—should look and act. And then our assessments begin to bear fruit.

Questions for Discussion and Reflection

1. Do you believe that God loves *you*?
2. What would happen to you if you walked into your local church building with the church bulletin in hand and looked up to see the Lord Himself seated on an elevated

throne, with His train of glory filling the building with light? How would you respond to His holy presence? Would you join Isaiah, feeling deep dread, regret, and shame in your heart because of hidden sins and the wrong words you've spoken in your life?

3. Have you been hit with the reality of how desperately you really do need God? What is your response? What should your response be?

4. Have you asked yourself the same question Jesus asked of the crippled man sitting by the water at the pool of Bethesda in John 5, "Do you want to get well?"

5. Have you faced the tough questions: *What started me on this descent of pain—how and where did I first begin to lose heart? What are the behaviors or sinful practices in my life that need to be purged? What attributes must be added because they are missing or in low supply in my life? Do I have a rich supply of the things Paul said should be present in abundance in a healthy Christian life that is controlled by the Spirit of God?*

Action Point: Assess the behaviors you need to eliminate. List those you want to add to your life. Start slowly, and keep at it even when you fail. Reward yourself for each victory. Call on God for help and thank Him when He answers!

· 11 ·

FINALLY AWARE
OF THE GREAT DESIRE
Opening the Door for True Intimacy
with God and Those We Love

Once you thoroughly assess your life, you become more *aware* of who you are. You see yourself before your righteous and holy God, and this births an awareness of something you lack, of something you *want*.

As you look inward, a greater level of self-awareness enters your life, opening the door for true intimacy with God and those you love. This is where you discover the great desire God has placed in your heart: "God, I so need You. . . . I am so desperate for You!" Suddenly the deep truths of John 15 come alive: "I am the true vine, and My Father is the vinedresser. . . . I am the vine, you are the branches. He who abides in Me, and I in him, bears much fruit; for without Me you can do nothing" (vv. 1, 5).

When we look at Jesus Christ, our living Vine, then glance

over the withered branches of our failure-scorched lives, we are tempted to give up. We're not up to this—it's too hard.

That is *exactly* the point! The Lord has been waiting for this moment. Now, *at last*, He can really do something in your life! This is when we pray, "God, I've been dead for a long time. Take me and replant me beside Your unfailing river of life" (see Rev. 22:1).

When God becomes our chief desire and primary meditation, we share the longing and the privilege of declaring the same promise the psalmist did in Psalm 1:3:

> He shall be like a tree
> Planted by the rivers of water,
> That brings forth its fruit in its season,
> Whose leaf also shall not wither;
> And whatever he does shall prosper.

✦ *You enter this surrender with your eyes on Christ,*
not on what you surrender.

Richard Foster penned a powerful piece in his book *Celebration of Discipline* that extols the emergence of "the people who know the spirit of Emanuel." He wrote: "We've seen it before, there are pockets of it still. But now Heaven and Earth are standing on tiptoes waiting. May *you* be one of His Spirit-led people."[1]

I would phrase it this way: Heaven and Earth are standing on tiptoes, awaiting the emergence of a Spirit-led, Spirit-intoxicated people—people who know the Spirit of *Emanuel*, which means "God with us." They are awaiting people whose God is as real to them as a cloud by day and a fire by night were to the children of Israel in the days of old. It is in this awareness stage of your journey back to the recovery of heart that you begin to learn the heavenly art of surrender. Your journey now looks like this:

Losing Heart: The Descent into Pain
Ambushed and Assaulted
Anger
Anxiety
Aloneness
Alienation
Arrogance
Adulteries of the Heart
Addiction
Recovery of Heart: Coming Out of Pain
Affection of God
Assessment
Awareness

True surrender begins in earnest very near the place where you hit bottom, but you enter this surrender with your eyes on Christ, not on what you surrender to Him.

All Pretense Is Gone

This is where you turn from your ways and allow your heart to cry out to God in brokenness: "Dad, will You forgive me? I'm sorry. I love You, Dad."

All pretense is gone.

Every well-worn defensive strategy has been laid aside.

Surrender is your road, and your goal is freedom with a pure heart.

You sing in harmony with the beloved psalmist who knew what it meant to fall, to fail, and to descend to the depths of human sinfulness. Singing through your tears and praying for mercy and grace to cover the missteps, you offer the Lord all of the sins, failures, and fears of a lifetime:

> Have mercy upon me, O God,
> According to Your lovingkindness;
> According to the multitude of Your tender mercies,
> Blot out my transgressions.
> Wash me thoroughly from my iniquity,
> And cleanse me from my sin.
> For I acknowledge my transgressions,
> And my sin is always before me.
> . . . Wash me, and I shall be whiter than snow.
> . . . Create in me a clean heart, O God,
> And renew a steadfast spirit within me.
> Do not cast me away from Your presence,
> And do not take Your Holy Spirit from me.
> Restore to me the joy of Your salvation,
> And uphold me by Your generous Spirit.
> . . . The sacrifices of God are a broken spirit,
> A broken and a contrite heart—
> These, O God, You will not despise.
>
> (Psalm 51:1–3, 7, 10–12, 17)

You Are on the Healing Path

"Dear Father, renew a right spirit within me": when you say that with all of your heart, you are on the healing path.

It involves so much more than going to church three times a week or serving on all of the ministry committees. Healing comes as you draw close to the Spirit of God. And the fruit of that intimate relationship becomes plain to all who know you.

Anything else amounts to religious self-help. This generally unfruitful category includes most of the behaviors and practices in our lives that spiritual surgery needs to remove. This is accomplished the old-fashioned way prescribed in the Scriptures: through confession of our sins one to another, and through genuine repentance and forgiveness. We can do all of these only through the grace and mercy of God.

Paul was careful to point out the difference between the brand of "repentance" that is little more than remorse over being caught and what he called "godly sorrow." He said, "For godly sorrow produces repentance leading to salvation, not to be regretted; but the sorrow of the world produces death" (2 Cor. 7:10).

Earlier in the same letter, Paul gave specific examples of compromise requiring genuine repentance:

> Do not be unequally yoked together with unbelievers. For what fellowship has righteousness with lawlessness? And what communion has light with darkness?
>
> And what accord has Christ with Belial? Or what part has a believer with an unbeliever?
>
> And what agreement has the temple of God with idols? For you are the temple of the living God. As God has said:
>
>> "I will dwell in them
>> And walk among them.
>> I will be their God,
>> And they shall be My people."
>
> Therefore
>
>> "Come out from among them
>> And be separate, says the Lord.
>> Do not touch what is unclean,
>> And I will receive you."

"I will be a Father to you,
And you shall be My sons and daughters,
Says the LORD Almighty."

Therefore, having these promises, beloved, let us cleanse ourselves from all filthiness of the flesh and spirit, perfecting holiness in the fear of God.

(2 Corinthians 6:14–7:1)

Avoid relationships, agreements, or close friendships that might negatively affect your impact on others. Be careful. If you find yourself in trouble, make some course corrections.

You must be willing to say no to *anything* in life that will keep you from God. One church leader from an African nation even turned away from marrying someone because the fiancée finally revealed that she had no intention of leaving her home nation in Europe to go on the mission field in Africa.

Procrastination may be one of the enemy's most effective tools in his assault on the children of God. We prefer to struggle through life for years, carrying around the two-hundred-pound monkey of past sin or unresolved conflict rather than take the hour, day, or week it might take to put the monkey where it belongs.

How many times have family members carried past offenses against each other, sometimes not speaking to one another for years, waiting until their final breaths in a hospital room to forgive one another and make up? What a waste! Would it be better to ditch the "monkey" of broken relationships and bitterness *today* so you can enjoy years of rich relationship in the future?

Many of us launch into this life pattern during our homework days in school. We put off the unpleasant homework and played with our friends . . . all the while carrying that silent dread: *Payday is coming when Mom finds out*. We carry that procrastination fascination with us into college, then the workplace. As many a spouse will testify, the procrastination virus has weakened many a marriage as well!

Whatever hinders you from obeying God and being transformed, it has to go. Whether it's credit cards, your reputation, success, security, ambition, or your favorite drug of choice, God is calling for a clean sweep.

✦ *God freely uses outward things to work
the inward process of your transformation.*

Many of our challenges may not be "evil" in and of themselves. But know that everything God desires requires obedience from the *heart*, and He freely uses outward things to work the inward process of your transformation.

Our Love of Shortcuts

The problem is that we like shortcuts too much. We seem always to be willing to bypass the purity of the heart needed to develop and support purity of outward performance. John Ortberg weighed in on this with his usual strength:

> Everybody knows that Christians should be different by being more loving and more joyful, and everybody knows that they're not. So don't we have to do something to be different? In other words, if we can't be holy, shouldn't we at least be weird?
>
> . . . That's why the Pharisees' religion became so noxious to people. It was because they weren't holy. They were not being authentically transformed, they were just weird. But they didn't know they were weird—they thought they were holy.

And in the person of Jesus, human beings who thought they were a million miles away from God finally saw somebody who was holy without being weird. And they'd do anything to get close to Him. They'd sell everything they had. They'd come pushing and shoving to have that kind of life.

And that's the life of which you and I are stewards. . . .

I believe that if people are serious about faith, but they don't experience authentic transformation in time, inevitably their spiritual life will deteriorate into the search for superficial boundary markers that will prop up their sense of being different from outsiders.[2]

Paul wrote,

For the love of Christ compels us, because we judge thus: that if One died for all, then all died; and He died for all that those who live should no longer live for themselves, but for Him who died for them and rose again. Therefore, from now on, we regard no one according to the flesh. Even though we have known Christ according to the flesh, yet now we know Him thus no longer. Therefore, if anyone is in Christ, he is a new creation; old things have passed away; behold, all things have become new.

(2 Corinthians 5:14–17)

The truth is we need a new breed. We are called to be holy and dedicated to service to our holy God. Paul said Jesus "gave himself for us, that he might redeem us from all iniquity, and purify unto himself a peculiar people, zealous of good works" (Titus 2:14 KJV). In fact, we read in Revelation 1:6 that Jesus "hath made us kings and priests unto God and his Father" (KJV). God is calling for nothing less than a radical transformation in every life surrendered to Him.

What practices keep you from an intimate relationship with God? Are you willing to give them up?

Now, I'm not asking you to be weird or fanatical. I'm simply asking, are you willing to say no to those things and say yes to God?

For those of us who know the pain near the bottom of the road to the loss of heart, we can relate to the man who gets diagnosed with diabetes and is told, "Suddenly you want to live a long life. Are you willing to give up these things that you can no longer handle?"

✦ *By the time he stepped into his father's embrace,*
he was a changed man.

A Radically New Life

I've mentioned the plight of the prodigal son who foolishly demanded his inheritance early, then squandered it on sinful pursuits. The Bible says this man woke up one day in a pigsty. It was a crushing discovery for this young rebel. As one writer put it:

> This is a very dangerous moment, when God seems set against everything that has meant life to us. Satan spies his opportunity, and leaps to accuse God in our hearts. *You see*, he says, *God is angry with you. He's disappointed in you. If he loved you he would make things smoother.* He's not out for your best, you know. The Enemy always tempts us back toward control, to recover and rebuild the false self. We must remember that it is out of love that God thwarts our imposter. As Hebrews reminds us, it is the son whom God disciplines, therefore do not lose heart. (12:5–6)[3]

We should be glad we serve a God who loves us enough to thwart the imposter who urges us to get angry at God when we should be grateful for His loving discipline.

When the prodigal son finally had clear understanding of his fallen position, he *did* something. He made an about-face and physically turned away from the pigsty and began walking home. By the time he stepped into his father's embrace, he was a changed man.

When this new awareness hits you, you delight in your heavenly Father's embrace. You will follow after Him all of the days of your life. He literally changes your habits and practices to reflect His glory and nature.

It is at the point of our repentance that God is always at His best. The late E. V. Hill once noted when Jesus talked with Peter at the seashore postresurrection, it was *after* Peter had denied the Lord three times. (Which was after Peter had promised Jesus, "I'll never deny You.")

Imagine what it was like for Peter to face Jesus after all of that! I can almost see Peter, shoulders pressed down with all of the weight of his failures, wiping away tears as he stood before his Savior. And Jesus looked directly into Peter's eyes and then asked, "Simon, son of Jonas, lovest thou me?" (John 21:16 KJV).

When God gives you a newfound awareness of your destiny through His presence, you may face the same questions that Jesus posed to Peter. It isn't necessarily because He is calling you to be an apostle or to die crucified upside down like Peter. It is because you are a redeemed child of God, with an eternal mandate to spread the Good News, unconditional love, and unending hope in Christ to everyone you encounter.

As one writer put it, we are called to "a radical life" in Christ, and that means we should become more fully ourselves and move into the hearts of others with a redemptive purpose:

A person who lives a radical life, on the other hand, who is on the healing path toward becoming more fully himself and more essentially like Jesus, moves into the hearts of others with a redemptive purpose: to expose depravity and draw forth dignity. We are all a mixture of dignity (that which deeply desires what is good, lovely, and true) and depravity (that which refuses to confess that God is the sole good, beauty, and truth that our heart was made to desire— Psalm 73:25). Redemptive conversation delights in all that reflects dignity and disrupts whatever reeks of depravity.[4]

It is time for the branch to follow in the path and purpose of the Vine. Once made aware of our royal lineage in the King, we can never ever properly step back into the role of pauper and foolish jester. Others are waiting to be pulled from the ditch we know only too well, and many of them are in our own house.

Questions for Discussion and Reflection

1. Have you honestly asked God to "renew a right spirit" within you? What does this mean? What would change in your life as a result of this right spirit?
2. Are you a procrastinator? In what areas of your life does procrastination manifest itself? What is holding you back from losing the two-hundred-pound monkey of past sin and unresolved conflict?
3. Are you willing to give them up? Are you willing to live a life of abandonment, to set aside everything that keeps you from walking a life with God?
4. Would it be better to ditch the "monkey" of broken relationships and bitterness *today* so you can enjoy years and years of rich relationship ahead of you?

Action Point: Choose one destructive habit, attitude, or action you have become aware of through this book. What "monkey" have you been carrying? Start leaving it behind by embracing hope: ask God to show you steps for unloading the monkey. Then take those steps, one day at a time.

· 12 ·

ATTACHED AND THRIVING

Embracing the Relationships
We Were Made For

The story of Jacob, the patriarch who wrestled with the Lord until the Lord blessed him, marks a pivotal moment in life. I pray it comes to us all, that defining moment when we realize how much we need God. This is when we understand that all the labors of our lives, and everything we have chased after, pale in comparison to Him.

The truth is that without Him, you can do nothing. When you have been washed, forgiven, kissed, held, and told that you mean everything to the One who loves you—and you *believe* it—it changes everything!

When you finally believe that God has forgiven you, has washed away your sin and failure, and that He really loves you, *then* you are ready to embrace the world—rough edges and all!

Acceptance in God arms you to cope with life and offer acceptance to others, even when reconnection means risk to you.

The Way Relationships Help and Heal

As I've said again and again, I am convinced that we are broken in relationships, and we are healed in our relationships. That is because our God and Maker created us *for* relationship with Him and others.

Once you really know who you are and are confident that God loves you exactly the way He made you, then you can embrace the Christlike lifestyle of loving others in all of their unloveliness and pain.

The Little League ballplayer whose allegedly adult coach beat him up verbally somehow comes roaring back to hit the game-winning home run! How did he do it? Did the motivation come from the wounded man taking out his childish anger on a boy half his size and a quarter of his age? No.

It was the man in the stands that boy calls "Dad." He is the one who hugged the boy between innings, then looked him in the eye and said, "Son, don't worry about the coach. I'll take care of him. It's going to be all right. You've got some serious game left in you, and it's time to let it out! Now, go back out there and let 'em have it!"

With one final glance at the smiling figure in the stands—that giant of a man who anchored his world—the Little Leaguer stepped to the mound, tapped the plate with his bat, stared the pitcher in the eye, and made the most important hit of his lifetime. As long as the son was attached, heart to heart, to his father, he could overcome.

Your journey now looks like this:

Losing Heart: The Descent into Pain
Ambushed and Assaulted
Anger
Anxiety
Aloneness
Alienation
Arrogance
Adulteries of the Heart
Addiction
Recovery of Heart: Coming Out of Pain
Affection of God
Assessment
Awareness
Attachments

Think of the husband who comes home tired and dejected after a rough day at work. The fire that fuels his competitive edge at the office is nearly snuffed out. Then his wife, who has worked a full day herself, says, "I understand, baby. You're still the man!" She hugs him and says, "I love you, no matter what." Is it any wonder that he goes to work early the next day, ready to charge hell with a water pistol? He is loved, so the obstacles just don't matter. It's hard to beat a man who knows he's already won.

These are portraits of healthy attachments in the midst of difficult circumstances. They are our lifelines, and they are God's gift to us.

Attachment Styles That Hurt Rather Than Help

The sad reality is that many of us have unhealthy "attachment styles" that strongly affect our lives and well-being. There appear to be four dominant styles, just one of which is helpful:

1. *The avoidant attachment style* leads you to move away from God when distressed. You turn instead to possessions, success, or other addictions. You are convinced that God just can't be trusted. Or you may express your anger toward God by plunging into sinful habits or by self-medicating your pain.

2. *The ambivalent attachment style* is marked by a tendency to waver between opinions or emotional states. You may feel rage toward God one moment, then feel as though you are drowning in self-incrimination and excessive self-blame the next. Your tendency is to search for a replacement attachment *figure* rather than for things or achievements to ease your pain.

3. *The disorganized attachment style* is a third unhealthy category in which you view every limit or boundary as a continuation of your "long history of loss." You may think God is malicious, "just like my other caregivers." Sometimes you might be described by others as "clingy and filled with rage," but you would say, "No, it is *God* who is seething with rage over *me*. My sorry life is simply something I deserve." Fearing something even *worse* might happen if you openly display your feelings, you tend to *bury* them, unaware that they will merely surface another way in the form of anxiety or even panic attacks.

4. *The secure attachment style* describes the ideal way we relate to God and to others. While you may feel the full range of emotions generated by loss or grief over unexpected crisis, you will tend to take the entire process to God in open, honest communication. You may spend hours or days asking God to tell you *why* a thing happened, feeling lonely, afraid, and vulnerable. But in the end, you will ultimately turn toward God and change your "why" to "how." In the end you ask, *"How do I go on?"*[1]

Fran Stott once said, "Every child needs at least one person who's crazy about him." I think that applies to "kids" of all ages. What would happen in your life if you knew God was crazy about you? What would change in your life if you had absolute assurance that God is fighting hell for your soul and well-being? Remember, you were created by a God who wants your heart! He has already done everything that must be done to save your soul. Now He is working out the salvation of your everyday life.

✦ *What would happen in your life if you knew God was crazy about you?*

According to Dr. Henry Cloud, the Lord does this through our relationships: "Relationship or bonding . . . is at the foundation of God's nature. Since we are created in His likeness, relationship is our most fundamental need, the very foundation of who we are. Without relationship, without attachment to God and others, we can't be ourselves."[2]

If you recall the principle of the branches being linked to

the Vine for maximum fruitfulness, then you may see the eternal *and* earthly value of finally being connected to God.

Without Him, None of Us Can Do Anything Worth Doing

It is healthy for you to recognize God's call and expectations in your life. Without Him, none of us can do anything worth doing. When we accept the way of Jesus, we begin to experience deep satisfaction.

The key is our understanding that because of His love for us, we can approach Him with a spirit of expectation. His abiding love soothes our troubled hearts. He can make a "bridge over troubled waters" if you will seek Him with all your heart.

Throughout His earthly lifetime, Jesus made His relationship with God His priority. And He expects the same of us today. Jesus said in Matthew 10:37, "Anyone who loves his son or daughter more than me is not worthy of me." Jesus wants to be the first link in the attachment chain. He wants us to turn first to Him, not to our parents or our spouses or anyone else. And when we do, our lives become properly ordered. In the words of C. S. Lewis, "Whenever we try to put second things into the first place position, we lose the joy of both God and whatever we are trying to replace Him with."[3]

I've used the term *attachment* several times in this chapter. *Attachment* refers to our closest relationships, those bonds with others that directly influence who we are, how we see ourselves, and how we relate to life and all of its ups and downs. We have all kinds of relationships in life, ranging from parent-child relationships to casual acquaintances: the baker on the corner, the policeman who directs us away from an accident, and the bank clerk who smiles at us through four inches of bulletproof glass.

There are five criteria or standards that, taken together, separate our *attachments* from other relationships in life:

The Five Criteria
for an Attachment Relationship

1. Proximity (closeness) to the caregiver is sought, especially in times of trouble.
2. The caregiver provides a safe haven, a felt sense of security.
3. The caregiver provides a secure base from which to explore the world.
4. Any threat of separation induces fear and anxiety.
5. Loss of the caregiver induces grief and sorrow.[4]

God Is the Ultimate Attachment Figure

As Dr. Sibcy and I noted in our book on the subject, *Attachments: Why You Do the Things You Do—The Secret to Healthy Relationships*, no one can take the place of our Creator in the attachment chain. God is the ultimate attachment figure. "In times of trouble, God can seem far away, but He isn't. He's always near, and He wants us to know that. He wants us to feel His embrace and to feel secure in Him. But although He's always close to us, when trouble strikes we either move closer or further away."[5]

✦ *Although He's always close to us, when trouble strikes we either move closer or further away.*

Psalm 46 has always been a source of comfort for me during times of adversity. Something lifts in my spirit every time I read the ancient truths:

> God is our refuge and strength
> A very present help in trouble.
> Therefore we will not fear,
> Even though the earth be removed,
> And though the mountains be carried into the midst of
>   the sea;
> Though its waters roar and be troubled,
> Though the mountains shake with its swelling.
>
> (Psalm 46:1–3)

In other words, He's there no matter what happens!

He is in the midst of it all and will never abandon or forsake us. He will see you through if you can learn to be still and know that He is God.

I've just described the fruit, or personal benefits, of developing an abiding relationship with God. Have you ever experienced these? These benefits come to you when you give the Lord top priority in your life.

God did not magically cease to be the center of our universe simply because Adam and Eve sinned in the Garden of Eden. He never ceased being who He was and is simply because we did. It isn't a matter of mankind re-creating God in its own image. No, the ball is in our court.

It is time for us to get back in joint and reconnect with our Source of all joy. Just as a youngster in the park returns to home base and touches Mom's knee or connects with her approving glance from time to time before venturing bravely to the next play area, our greatest security in life comes when we "check in with Daddy." When we build on our attachment to God—when we turn to Him for guidance and comfort in the ordinary junctures of life—God is our secure base. He's the foundation from which we confidently explore our world.[6]

This attachment to our heavenly Father also models the ideal attachment relationship for every other important relationship in our lives. It ultimately strengthens, purifies, and preserves our attachments to spouses, family members, and other trusted attachment figures. The joy of the Lord is our strength.

Why is this so important? It is because these other attachments—the *horizontal* or earthly attachments with other people—are also meant to provide crucial nutrients for healthy living in an unhealthy world. "God is our principle attachment figure. But we still need others. In fact, we know that God has brought those relationships into our lives to provide, in an earthly setting, what God wants us to have. But when we're in trouble, we know to turn to God first. He is the One 'who sticks closer than a brother' "[7] (Proverbs 18:24).

A. W. Tozer wrote: "The Bible is not an end in itself, but a means to bring men to an intimate and satisfying knowledge of God, that they may enter into Him, that they may delight in His presence, may taste and know the inner sweetness of the very God Himself in the core and center of their hearts."[8] If we don't understand that, we move Christ to the back room of our lives and proceed as if we don't really need Him in the kitchen or workplace.

Distractions from My Primary Attachment

I spent the majority of my life, including the years I labored through my doctoral studies at the College of William & Mary in Virginia, memorizing psychological theory to help others. In fact, at one point in my life, I probably became more enamored with counseling techniques and strategies than I was with the great work of God in human lives.

I'm not proud of it, but in a way I lost sight of the power of God while trying to figure out why people do the things they do. While I deeply value the education I received, God calls us to believe Him for our lives as well as for our eternal salvation.

> ✦ *I lost sight of the power of God while trying to figure out why people do the things they do.*

How do you press on when your legs get knocked out from underneath you and life just isn't the way it's supposed to be? You return to the relationship with the One who created you in the first place.

The excellent book, *Hope When You're Hurting*, says: "The soul will not be healed without relationship. It was in the context of relationship that we felt most abandoned, violated, and ashamed. It will be in the midst of relationship that we begin to taste the wonder of connection, intimacy, and forgiveness."[9]

The book continues, "Many of our problems are uniquely *human* problems, that is, they reflect our struggle to live as people who were meant to enjoy perfect community in a world where there is none. And these problems will not be addressed richly or deeply apart from community. Until the sufferer deals with his problems in a relationship with someone else, there is really no hope." [10]

Attachment Is at the Core of Freedom from Addiction

If you've passed down the road of pain through assault, anger, anxiety, alienation, arrogance, adulteries of the heart, and addiction, you need more than some bright idea to restore your heart. In fact, I don't believe that you can really overcome addiction in your life without healthy attachment.

Again, I'm not talking about mere close relationships. Healing comes when you get into healthy bonds with God and other people. When Christian counselors work with men addicted to pornography or those who fell into illicit affairs, the usual counseling techniques apart from attachments with God and others just don't work. Healing is rooted in intimacy-oriented therapy.

✦ *Healing comes when you get into*
healthy bonds with God and other people.

Treatments avoiding close attachments help addicted people change their behavior for a season. Some programs promote recognition of a Higher Power, and I'm thankful for that. But often it isn't enough to set the addict free.

Religion without relationship produces greater discipline and more good deeds, but it cannot lead us to recovery of the heart. That comes through intimate relationship with God and with the people He places in our lives.

What is intimacy? Think of it this way: *in-to-me-see*. True, healthy intimacy begins *vertically*. First we reestablish honest communication with God. That, in turn, opens the door to building intimate and productive relationships with other people. Only then will recovery of the heart really take place.

Dr. Sibcy and I noted, "Again and again in our practice we have seen that when clients work on strengthening and, as needed, healing, their relationship with their Creator they soon begin to see noticeable changes in their attachment relationships with others. The result is akin to a whole new start on life and the joys it offers."[11]

While researching and writing the book *Why You Do the Things You Do*, we found that when people miss the relational component in healthy living, especially the absolute need for a genuine attachment to God, then they never really grasp the value of relationships.

It isn't enough to tell hurting people, "Make sure you perform all the appropriate religious duties: go to church, don't smoke, don't drink, and make sure you date good people." These are all good things to do, and God's Word mandates some of them. But the God who pursues always looks at the heart. He has never been impressed by the good deeds of someone whose heart is far from Him. Jesus said His Father searches the earth for those "who will worship . . . in spirit and truth" (John 4:23).

As Dr. Gary Smalley put it in his book *The DNA of Relationships:* "Life is relationships; the rest is just details. God made you for relationships. You can't change that. You can work either with or against this DNA, but you can't choose whether it exists. The only choice you have is whether you will work to make those relationships great or allow them to cause you—and others—great pain."[12]

✦ *Life is relationships; the rest is just details.*

Life really is bundled in our relationships with God and one another. Too many of us get lost in the details and miss the most important part. Pain seems to constantly pull us back to the most essential part of life.

We Find Our Healing in Our Divine Healer

Recently I worked with a missionary who was suffering from the loss of his dream. He told me about the miraculous beginnings of his ministry overseas, how he overcame impossible odds to launch his ministry. He faithfully served the Lord and the people in Bangladesh for sixteen years, building hospitals and leading many people to the Lord. Then the day came when a woman suddenly turned her vehicle right in front of his car without warning.

She was critically injured in the accident. He learned she was a high-ranking official in Bangladesh, and he knew—completely apart from his desire that she recover—that he would be blamed if she died.

As he told me how he prayed at her bedside, he started weeping. "Tim, I prayed to God for her. You don't know how I wept by her bedside, praying that God would save her life! And He didn't."

He was right. Through a series of painful events, this faithful missionary and his wife were forced to return to the United States. His missionary journey was over, his dream dead. Unfortunately, his journey into pain had just begun.

It seemed that nobody wanted an old missionary. He felt like a stranger when he came home. So he and his wife disappeared in the cocoon of their house for years. "We were lost, Tim," he said. "I just didn't believe there was any hope for me anymore."

I interviewed this man during a live national radio broadcast, and at one point his pain just overwhelmed him. He cried, and I think everyone listening joined him. Finally he looked at me and said, "Tim, pray for me. Do you think there's a place for me now?"[13]

As with the Israelites in captivity, God heard his groanings. This man and his wife found their hope in God, and with the help of other caring believers, they are currently coming out of their pain.

We find our healing in our Healer. We recover our joy in Him who *is* joy incarnate. We recover our broken lives in the One who is the way, the truth, and the life. It is time to open our hearts to Him and believe in the transforming power of Jesus Christ.

Attachment to God Is All

The exciting, sold-out world conferences on Christian counseling, like those sponsored by the American Association of Christian Counselors (AACC) every other year in Nashville, are valuable forums for teaching people sound counseling techniques and strategies and delivering information about emerging clinical issues. But if we miss the pattern, the power, and the way of God in this life, we have missed it all. There is nothing else.

> ✦ *If we miss the pattern, the power, and the way
> of God in this life, we have missed it all.*

Attachments are so essential to God's plan for man that He uses them constantly in our daily lives:

God sets us up for encounters that have the potential to change our lives. Some encounters are surprising but expected, as in significant conversations with a spouse or good friend. Others are serendipitous rendezvous that leave us with a sense of destiny and wonder. Not every person or every conversation is meant to be life changing. If we attempted to make every conversation deep and eternally important, we would get little done and be a nuisance to most people we meet. Instead, we are to live with openness (faith) and expectancy (hope), invested in giving and receiving (love) from others as God so moves us.[14]

A Remarkable Companion of God in Terrible Circumstances

John Ortberg tells the story of a friend who met a remarkable woman named Mabel in a life-changing encounter. This friend counseled patients at a state-run convalescent hospital populated mostly by victims of senility, dementia, and severe physical challenges.

One day he saw an old woman strapped up in a wheelchair whose face was an absolute horror. He told my friend John: "She had an empty stare, and the white pupils of her eyes told me she was blind; and the large hearing aid over one ear indicated she was almost deaf. Cancer had eaten away one side of her face."

Mabel was eighty-nine years old and had been bedridden, blind, nearly deaf, and totally alone in that dark place for twenty-five years. He said, "I don't know why I spoke to her. She seemed less likely to respond than most of the people in that hallway." When he gave her a flower, she tried to smell it and then said, "Thank you, it's lovely. But can I give it to someone else? I can't see it, you know. I'm blind." When she spoke, her words were somewhat garbled because of her deformity.

The man said, "Of course" and guided her wheelchair down the hallway to another patient. Mabel held out the flower and said to the lady, "This is from Jesus."

The man later told John, "That was when it began to dawn on me that this [was] not an ordinary human being." He wheeled Mabel back to her room and as they talked, he discovered that she had grown up on a small farm that she managed with her mom. When her mother died, Mabel ran the farm alone until 1950, when her sickness and blindness sent her to the convalescent hospital.

Mabel shared her room with three roommates who were incoherent. They screamed occasionally but never talked, and they often soiled their bedclothes. When the man asked Mabel, "What do you think about when you lay here?" she said, "I think about my Jesus. . . . I think about how good He's been to me."

The man befriended Mabel and visited her once or twice a week for the next three years. She could recite long Bible passages from memory—word for word—and she knew all of the words to the old hymns. Mabel never spoke of loneliness or pain, and she seemed to be more of a blessing to John's friend than the other way around.

John said, "Mabel had something that you and I don't have much of. . . . She had extraordinary power. Lying in that bed, unable to see, unable to walk, unknown, unseen, unremembered—God looked down on Mabel from heaven and said, 'That is what a human life can be.' " [15]

The story reminds us of the absolute power released through our attachment to God. He helps us overcome every obstacle and wound in this life.

Pain may blind our eyes and confuse our thinking, but when we enter into intimate relationship with the Father, when we get attached to our Creator, we can simultaneously experience two emotions: sorrow and joy. In His presence, we don't fight *for* victory, we fight *from* victory.

Questions for Discussion and Reflection

1. Have you come to that "wrestling match" with God as Jacob did, that radical moment in life when you realize how much you need Him?
2. Do you believe you have been washed, forgiven, kissed, held, and told that you mean everything to the One who loves you? Do you really *believe* it?
3. Are you attached to your Father heart to heart? Describe how you are connected to your Father and what that means to you.
4. What would happen in your life if you knew that God was crazy about you? What would change in your life if you had absolute assurance that God literally is fighting hell for your soul and well-being?
5. Remember the fruits and personal benefits of developing an abiding relationship with God, particularly that He is a secure attachment figure no matter what happens. Have you ever experienced this in your life? How? If not, why?

Action Point: Identify someone with whom you'd like to form a healthy, life-giving attachment. Choose someone who loves God and exudes happiness and hope. See if that person would mentor you spiritually by meeting once a week for conversation, guidance, and prayer.

· 13 ·

ACTION REQUIRED
Converting Good Intentions into Godly Action

For many years during Michael Jordan's stellar career with the NBA, millions of young boys (and their dads) wanted to be just like Mike. Then along came Tiger, prowling the world's golf courses with a quietly aggressive and often dramatic play style. Millions of golf fans and would-be PGA champions dreamed of playing like Tiger Woods.

You often take on the character of the people with whom you spend time. When I spit, my son, Zach, spits. I clown around; he clowns around.

When you spend time in God's presence, His divine life begins to flow through you. Paul the apostle told us in Ephesians 5:1, "Be ye therefore followers of God as dear children" (KJV). Surround yourself with people who follow the Lord and who will pull you even higher. Paul told the Corinthians, "Imitate me, just as I also imitate Christ" (1 Cor. 11:1).

People in competitive business and sports environments seem to understand the need for mentors, coaches, and role models. They pay top money to spend time with people who "are doing it better than anybody else." Why? They want to learn or "catch" whatever it is that makes these top performers excel above the crowd.

Unfortunately, there seems to be a component in human nature that likes to follow another common saying: "Birds of a feather flock together." When we feel angry about something, we often seek out *other angry people* and conduct an anger meeting to *really* get hot about things!

Many of the top songs in one popular genre of music are fueled by the very common actions of people who feel depressed or "blue." I'm talking about the form of pop tunes called "crying-in-your-beer songs." It is true that many people head for a bar to soothe their sorrows with alcoholic drinks and a sympathetic listener across the bar or on the bar stool next to them.

Miserable people often feel more comfortable with other miserable people, just as people with low self-esteem often seek out other people with even lower self-esteem. Jesus described the problem two thousand years ago, saying, "They are blind leaders of the blind. And if the blind leads the blind, both will fall into a ditch" (Matt. 15:14).

Unfortunately, the practice of seeking solace from people who are as bad off as we are usually makes everything even worse! These relationships rarely if ever present genuine solutions to our problems, and in most cases, they are likely to perpetuate our problems.

Some folks avoid this trap only to fall into another one that is almost as common. They find themselves attracted to people who present seemingly brilliant *verbal* solutions to their problems but offer few results.

Most people can talk the talk. In fact, they'll talk and keep on talking while you lie dying. Other people—only *some*—can actually walk the walk. These folks understand the power of action over inaction.

You can teach a boy how to catch a baseball, but when is the lesson cemented into the brain? It's when he's in the bottom of the sixth inning, the bases are loaded, and the ball is hit to him at second base at eighty miles an hour. That's when it gets scary. And that is when head and heart come together. It's called *emotional learning*, and that is when training is converted to *action*.

That is what God does to us: He takes us on a journey to reunite head and heart and release His glory through our godly actions on earth.

You've reached a new stage on your journey:

Losing Heart: The Descent into Pain
Ambushed and Assaulted
Anger
Anxiousness
Aloneness
Alienation
Arrogance
Adulteries of the Heart
Addiction
Recovery of Heart: Coming Out of Pain
Affection of God
Assessment
Awareness
Attachments
Action

If good intentions and ideas automatically produced action, this world would be so cluttered with grand inventions, handy devices, and great architectural wonders that there wouldn't be room to turn around. Unfortunately, most of our good intentions and brilliant ideas die and are buried with us in all their unfulfilled glory. Why? They're missing the all-important component of *action*.

Paul the apostle was an *action* man. Although he was intellectually brilliant and could match minds with the best of them, he knew the value of action. He told the Christians in Philippi: "Those things, which ye have both learned, and received, and heard, and seen in me, *do*: and the God of peace shall be with you" (Phil. 4:9 KJV).

I love that *action* word Paul slapped right in the middle of his command to action: *do*. I'm referring to the life of faith lived out every day in practical ways. Somehow, the urgency I've sensed in Paul's words seems to have rubbed off on me. After working with thousands of clients and dealing with such serious problems for decades, there's a part of me that demands action when lives are on the line!

It Is Time for Action, Not Mere Talk

I wrote this book, for instance, from the collective blood, sweat, and tears of all the lives I've seen ravaged by brokenness, sorrow, fear, and despair. The pain that is overwhelming so many people in twenty-first-century America is out of control! It is time for action, not mere talk.

Nobody put it better than Bishop T. D. Jakes when he addressed thousands of Christian counselors at the AACC "Live the Life" World Conference in 2003:

I pastor in the inner city, and I was not raised in the inner city. I was not an at-risk youth. I was not raised by drug addicts or prostitutes, nor did I come from a broken home.

But I found myself in a situation where I'm pastoring and dealing with people who have problems so horrendous that they make my knees buckle sometimes when they tell me what's going on in their lives.

And I would love to report to you that it's just in the inner city. But I've been in the suburbs too. I've been in the homes of the rich and famous, and I've seen them facing crises just as big as those faced by people in the inner city. We've got a real thief loose in the darkness of this life that we really need to deal with. The problem has reached epidemic stage.[1]

I am going for nothing less than healing and total restoration of broken hearts—I have no time to write coffee table books. I'm declaring that God is out to help hurting people truly break free to something new. Are you ready to pay the price God asks *in action?*

Do What the Doctor Says

After you go to the doctor with serious symptoms of heart problems, blood sugar imbalances, or breathing difficulties, you *do what the doctor says.* Why? Because you are serious about getting well and getting on with your life.

The book *The Great Divorce* painted a vivid picture of action following assessment and attachment. A "ghost-man" encountered an angel and received a second chance to enter heaven. This ghost had a little red lizard sitting on his shoulder that twitched its tail like a whip and whispered sinful things into the ghost's ear. The ghost then snarled at the lizard and told it to shut up. Nevertheless, the lizard just wagged its tail and continued its whispering.

Finally, when the ghost-man turned away from the bright horizon where heaven was waiting, a bright angelic figure asked him if he was going, and why so soon:

> "Yes, I'm off," said the Ghost. "Thanks for all your hospitality. But it's no good, you see. I told this little chap" (here he indicated the Lizard) "that he'd have to be quiet if he came—which he insisted on doing . . . but he won't stop. I shall just have to go home."
>
> "Would you like me to make him quiet?" said the flaming Spirit—an angel, as I now understood.
>
> "Of course I would."
>
> "Then I will kill him," said the Angel, taking a step forward.[2]

The ghost-man feared the severity of the angel's idea and, after going back and forth in fear and double-mindedness, he finally faced his last chance.

> "Have I your permission?" said the Angel to the Ghost.
>
> "I know it will kill me."
>
> "It won't. But supposing it did?"
>
> "You're right. It would be better to be dead than to live with this creature."
>
> "Then I may?"
>
> ". . . Blast you! Go on, can't you? Get it over. Do what you like!" bellowed the Ghost; but ended, whimpering, "God help me. God help me."[3]

The angel grabbed the lizard and snapped it in half, and an amazing transformation took place. The ghost-man began to look less like a ghost and more like a real man by the minute. As for the lizard, it was transformed into a great stallion that then transported the restored man into the heavenly realm.

God has a way of taking the things we surrender to Him and transforming them into vehicles that transport us to new realms.

In *Every Case*, Action Is Required

We give up alcoholism and He anoints us to help set other alcoholics free in His name. We surrender our fears and He uses our testimonies to help free others trapped in their fears. We give Him a broken marriage and he sends out husband and wife as a team united to save other marriages at risk!

In *every case*, action is required. If you've ever tried to put together a bicycle or large toy for your child, you are familiar with the innocent phrase hidden somewhere on the box that takes three men to carry: "Assembly required."

God has given us everything we need for success in this life, but be sure you read the bold declarations appearing throughout His Word: *Action required.*

There are three provisions necessary to uphold us on this action journey with God to restore our hearts:

1. Vision
Proverbs 29:13 says, "The poor man and the oppressor have this in common: / The LORD gives light to the eyes of both." You must be able to see where you're going. One of the essential problems the Israelites faced was their inability to organize their lives and purposes under God's direction. When they did this, they prospered.

2. *Courage*

Jesus said, "Take up your cross and follow Me" (see Matt. 16:24). It takes courage to follow Christ, but He is also the Source of courage. It is God's component of hope as we take steps of obedience with well-directed determination.

3. *Competence*

This word describes all of the practical disciplines, skills, knowledge, guidelines, and instruction provided in God's Word and through diligent human study and skill development.

Training vs. "Trying"

John Ortberg maintains that we must *train* ourselves to run the race for Christ, based on Paul's instruction to the Corinthian believers:

> There is a real critical distinction between training and trying that I want to point out from Scripture. In 1 Corinthians 9:24, Paul says, "Do you not know that in a race the runners all compete but only one receives the prize? Run in such a way that you may win the prize." Then he notes that athletes enter training in all things.
>
> Here's the distinction—there's a enormous difference between *training* to do something [and] *trying* to do something.
>
> What does it mean to train? To train means you arrange your life around those activities that will enable you to do what you cannot now do by direct effort. As a general rule, if transformation is to take place on any significant sphere in a human life, it will require training, not just trying.
>
> Human beings tend to tremendously overestimate the

power of trying and underestimate the power of training. . . .

Paul told Timothy, "Train yourself unto godliness." Jesus said in Luke 6:40, "No disciple is above the master, but every disciple when fully trained will be like the master." Discipleship is a life of training.[4]

The Power of the Disciplines

Ron Hawkins, a mentor and very close friend, often shared about personal discipline and "the disciplines." In practicing spiritual behaviors such as prayer, solitude, rest, searching out the Scriptures, praise and worship, and kindness, he taught, we experience God, know that He is, and know that He loves us.

> ✦ *It is through the disciplines that we realize God is our safe haven and our secure base.*

A discipline helps teach us how to rely on Him so that in times of crisis we do it automatically, like breathing. This will help us break free of addictions that block our relationship with God. It is through the disciplines that we realize God is our safe haven and our secure base.

The most basic Christian disciplines include corporate worship, Bible reading, prayer, and fasting. Additional disciplines include searching the Scriptures (this is more than casual reading), establishing times of solitude and silence with God in order to listen to His voice, simplifying our lifestyles, keeping our successes and good deeds *secret*, developing the ability to talk to God constantly in simple prayer throughout our day, and meditation.[5] (Richard Foster defines meditation as "the ability to hear God's voice and obey His Word.")

Following are some more disciplines and details about them:

Obedience

Paul the apostle provided an incredibly detailed description of what is included in the obedient Christian life in his letter to the Ephesians. Just reading these verses will strengthen and enlighten your understanding of the role of obedience in the Christian walk:

> Put off, concerning your former conduct, the old man which grows corrupt according to the deceitful lusts, and be renewed in the spirit of your mind, and that you put on the new man which was created according to God, in true righteousness and holiness.
>
> Therefore, putting away lying, "Let each one of you speak truth with his neighbor," for we are members of one another. "Be angry, and do not sin": do not let the sun go down on your wrath, nor give place to the devil.
>
> Let him who stole steal no longer, but rather let him labor, working with his hands what is good, that he may have something to give him who has need.
>
> Let no corrupt word proceed from your mouth, but what is good for necessary edification, that it may impart grace to the hearers.
>
> And do not grieve the Holy Spirit of God, by whom you were sealed for the day of redemption. Let all bitterness, wrath, anger, clamor, and evil speaking be put away from you, with all malice. And be kind to one another, tenderhearted, forgiving one another, even as God in Christ forgave you.
>
> Therefore be imitators of God as dear children. And

walk in love. . . . Walk as children of light . . . finding out
what is acceptable to the Lord.

(Ephesians 4:22–5:1–2, 8, 10)

Notice the final phrase: "finding out what is acceptable to
the Lord." Do you know what is acceptable to the Father? It is
more than a list of "do nots." It is *doing* exactly what Jesus modeled when He walked among us. He *obeyed*. He avoided the "do
nots" and He put into *action* the "do's" of the Word.

Obedience is doing exactly what you're told, doing it immediately, and doing it with the right heart attitude.

Boldness

Bishop T. D. Jakes believes transformed Christians are bold
Christians. He said in a live address:

I believe in fightin' my way back! I'm not much of a wimp
and a crybaby, and I'm not a whiney, sour-faced, sissified
Christian who won't fight back. You can count on me to
knuckle at you two or three times if you come against me.

The Bible says the kingdom suffers violence and the violent take it by force. If you're going to have a life, you have
to fight for it. If you're going to have a family, you have to
fight for it.

If you are going to have any type of ministry or find your
purpose in life, you have to be prepared to fight for it. Because there is a thief who wants to strip you and wound you
and leave you half dead.[6]

Friendliness

Ovid said, "To be loved, be lovable." God's Word takes it a
step higher, describing the ideal friend this way: "There is a
friend who sticks closer than a brother" (Prov. 18:24). Now *that*
is a friend indeed. Jesus said it even better:

This is My commandment, that you love one another as I have loved you. Greater love has no one than this, than to lay down his life for his friends.

You are My friends if you do whatever I command you.

No longer do I call you servants, for a servant does not know what his master is doing; but I have called you friends, for all things that I heard from My Father I have made known to you.

(John 15:12–15)

When the Lord is as crazy about us as He is, we should be secure enough to be kind toward others. Our open-hearted love toward others is perhaps God's greatest advertisement in our love-starved world. Being kind, tenderhearted, and forgiving is inherently therapeutic. Make a short list of those you need to reach out to right now. A phone call, a short note, or even a gentle word asking for or offering forgiveness could heal a lot of pain.

Positivity

Employ the powerful discipline of the positive word. Dr. J. M. Gottman developed the Gottman Ratio from researching communication between married couples. He learned that it takes five positive interactions to overcome one negative statement or interaction. Since our cynical culture seems to excel at the art of the put-down, it seems we have much work to do. It is time to build up and encourage others with the discipline of the kind and uplifting word.[7]

Of course, God's Word revealed this principle long before Dr. Gottman ever entered the earthly scene. The Bible says, "Heaviness in the heart of man maketh it stoop: but a good [encouraging] word maketh it glad" (Prov. 12:25 KJV).

Tap the Positive Side of Anger

We've already examined the nature of anger, noting that it is a God-given emotion and a natural response to crisis or a threat. It is a response meant to recover that which was lost—an anger of hope.

Neil Clark Warren has a unique way of showing us the positive side of anger, when we use it the way God always intended.

> We need to have in our head pictures of an angry person who goes out and takes on a very difficult issue in the world. For instance, Lee Ioccoca said that when he saved the Chrysler Motor Company, "It was because we got so angry." And then he specifically talked about how angry he got with the *Wall Street Journal.*
>
> He said the *Wall Street Journal* article had asked, "Why don't you allow the Chrysler Motor Company to die with dignity?" He took the article to all of his suppliers. Then he took it to the other executives at Chrysler. Together, he said, they got angry enough to come up with the solutions that eventually saved the Chrysler Motor Company.
>
> Then Ioccoca said, "You know, there is no problem in the world today which, if we could get angry enough about it, we couldn't solve."
>
> And that is the kind of picture I want us to have in our heads. Of persons who have tremendous physiological preparedness to do something about the primary pain sources in their lives. That is anger . . . turned in the direction of wonderful service to the human race.[8]

Actions Must Follow Your Choices

You must build a bridge between *thinking about* action and actually beginning to *move* in the right direction. You must choose to grow in your relationship with your heavenly Father. Actions must follow your choices, and these actions become the force that will turn your life around.

Change vs. Growth

When we talk about change, it often sounds harsh to those listening: "Change your attitude." "Change your tone."

If you ask a roomful of people what comes to mind when they hear the term *change*, they will likely respond: "Change is tough. It's painful—no one likes it." It's true—change can be both tough and painful, but what happens to your view of change if you look at it as growth?

If you asked that same roomful of people what they think of when they hear the term *growth*, they would probably say: "Growth makes you stronger," or "Growth is like flowers blooming," or "You gain wisdom when you grow. Growth is a good thing."

So perhaps we should think of action and change as growth.

Preparing for Action

Counselors have found that a five-stage process occurs when we take action.[9] The process varies according to the individual and each set of circumstances.

Stage 1: Precontemplation

At this early stage, a person has little desire for change and may not even believe change is necessary.

Stage 2: Contemplation

In this phase, a person realizes that he needs to change but may not be convinced enough to exert the effort to do so. The person is still weighing the pros and cons of taking steps to change. (It is said that people can spend years in this stage.)

Stage 3: Preparation

At this stage, the person has made the decision to begin working toward his goals within one month's time. Technically, he's "done" nothing except make a commitment and intend to carry out a plan of action.

Stage 4: Action

This is where a person *takes action*. It doesn't matter whether the action is in the form of outward behavior (e.g., he stops drinking and starts praying) or inward behavior (e.g., he establishes a healthy thought life and uses positive thinking). The results of this stage are obvious: observable change takes place.

Stage 5: Maintenance

In counseling, this is called a *posttreatment program*, and it is designed to solidify the actions and positive changes that have taken place. In essence, the maintenance stage is concerned with preventing relapse—or another loss of heart.

Action Goals

Your central personal goal is to improve how you think, feel, and act in a goal-directed way. As we said before, *real change is observable!* Jesus put it this way: "The good man out of the good treasure of his heart brings forth what is good; and the evil man out of the evil treasure brings forth what is evil; for his mouth speaks from that which fills his heart" (Luke 6:45 NASB).

Goals serve as useful tools to help us put *action* behind our decisions. And goals are most useful if they match the needs we have at different phases of our lives.

Proverbs 27:19 says, "As in water face reflects face, / So the heart of a man reflects a man" (NASB). To grow, we must honestly assess where we are while also gaining an accurate picture of the resources available and the specific barriers we must overcome to achieve our goals.

The Bible reveals that many of the primary issues we face in life are related to brokenness in our relationship with God and others. Our wounds affect our core relational beliefs about God, about self, about others, and even the world around us. It is easier to see how short-term goals are linked to God's design if we understand that our emotions and life goals are directly tied to our sense of safety and stability in our relationships with God and others.

To establish healthy goals, we need to think clearly and according to God's Word. Paul described people who don't think this way when he said in Ephesians 4:18, "They are darkened in their understanding and separated from the life of God because of the ignorance that is in them due to the hardening of their hearts" (NIV). Perhaps 2 Corinthians 10:5 best explains God's prescribed short-term goals when we are combating destructive thoughts: "We demolish arguments and every pretension that sets itself up against the knowledge of God, and we take captive every thought to make it obedient to Christ" (NIV).

Tips for Establishing an Action Plan for Recovery of Heart

Write It Out

Some people never write out their action plans because they are convinced the effort is pointless. They might tell you, "It's all written in my head."

If you feel that way, you might find yourself in the same shoes as the friend who decided to renovate a bathroom in his home. The job took five times longer to complete than it should have because he had to make *seven* trips to the hardware store. He kept forgetting to purchase materials because they had slipped from the list "written in his head"!

Obviously, had this friend written out his action plan and developed a materials list ahead of time, he could have avoided such wastes of time. The same is true for you.

The discipline of writing your plan helps you assess any resources or help you might need to produce desired change in your life. As you begin, remember to keep your plan anchored in the Scriptures. We should be as dependent on God's Word as we are on food and water. The Scriptures literally are the food and water of spiritual life, and the only resource that we should constantly tap to grow in Christian maturity—and to recover our hearts.

List the behaviors you want to get rid of and those you want to start. As you do, consider also your relationships. Make a grid and think in these categories:

+ Spiritual
+ Relational
+ Physical
+ Emotional
+ Financial

+ Social
+ Cognitive

Begin with Short-Term Goals

These should be goals you can attain in a relatively short period of time (ten weeks or less). "Small" successes keep you motivated to make bigger ones. Though short-term goals may be only a small portion of your growth and recovery, the change they form will probably feel dramatic!

For example, the following "small" things will probably make a *big* difference in how you feel:

+ Set aside a few minutes every day for Bible reading and prayer.
+ Talk to a friend, counselor, or pastor about what's bothering you. Schedule a meeting time with this person once a week.
+ Lose three pounds by eating better and exercising more (pack a healthy lunch and exercise twenty minutes a day—if your doctor permits).
+ Catch up on sleep, and begin getting eight hours of sleep a night.
+ Begin attending a weekly church small group.
+ Do three things you *enjoy* by next Tuesday.
+ Stop talking down to yourself, and start treating yourself with love.
+ Find one way to help someone this week.
+ Forgive others, even if they don't deserve it.
+ Forgive yourself, even if you don't feel you deserve it.
+ Quit the unhealthy thing you're addicted to (and get help to stay free from it).
+ Be kinder to your family; spend more time with your children.

Focus on Finding Solutions

Sometimes the magnitude of our problems makes us feel overwhelmed. What do you do when everything seems bad and looks as if it's getting worse? If you are feeling stuck and can't break free, seek out appropriate medical assistance and professional Christ-centered counseling. God does awesome work in the lives of those who boldly take these steps to get help.

For every problem you have, look for the built-in strengths you have and make them a starting line for improvement and growth. Don't look past the negatives to the point you ignore dangerous situations. But do focus on creating a valid list of positive strengths. They form the seeds from which you will blossom and reap all the benefits of growth.

Scan the following examples, and notice that for each problem there is also a strength that may produce measurable improvement:

Problem	Strength
Some people have been very abusive and taken advantage of me.	There are people near you who love and will help you.
My son is failing his classes.	Your son is still attending classes!
My spouse and I fight every day.	You and your spouse are still together, and you are still talking.
My family is an emotional and spiritual wreck.	Although your family has been going through so much, you are still going!
I have been a sinner my entire life.	You have forgiveness through your sins through Christ— now you have a new life!
I feel so miserable and guilty.	You are able to feel emotions, you have a sense of right and wrong, and you want to live a good life. That's good!

I am too old and too fat.

> You are still alive and it is
> never too late to change!

I am so tired.

> You are trying very hard, but
> take time to rest as well.
> (Even God rested!)

Base your solutions upon your strengths. Make them stronger, and let them constructively compete with and replace the problems in your life. In the process of change, you inevitably find and master new skills to complement those you already have.

Action Planning: The Details

A formal plan of action takes strategies for accomplishing goals and divides them into workable objectives. It puts them in a feasible order and assigns key milestones and realistic completion dates for each objective on the road to an ultimate goal.

Here are more good reasons to formulate a plan of action.

A Plan Improves Discipline

It takes a great deal of discipline to move from contemplation to action. A formal action plan effectively holds you accountable because the plan is concrete. It confronts you with its simple, daily, and unavoidable question: Did you follow the plan, or didn't you?

A Plan Prevents Overwhelming Feelings

The path from where you are now to a desired destination or goal is often an uphill route strewn with debris and obstacles of all kinds. A clear plan makes the road seem less overwhelming because it provides a step-by-step solution.

When developed correctly, a good plan of action has many small and manageable objectives on the way to accomplishing major goals. This goes a long way to remove or lessen the dramatic feelings that often descend on us when we are tackling large projects or problems.

A Plan Improves Action Strategies

Often when you begin to put your plan down on paper, you discover new insights that lead to improved strategies to accomplish your goals.

A Plan Helps You Access the Practicality of Goals

Just as you often find improved action strategies when you create an action plan, you may also discover ways to alter your goals to make them more feasible, appropriate, and practical.

A Plan Helps You Identify Potential Obstacles

It is difficult to overcome an obstacle you haven't seen or anticipated. The purposeful, step-by-step thinking that goes into developing an action plan often uncovers or anticipates the many things that may become obstacles to your original plan. As you identify obstacles, modify your plan to accommodate them.

A Plan Helps You Manage Post-Decision Depression

G. Egan describes post-decision depression as "the angst that comes from wondering whether one has made the right decision."[10] Whether you decide to stop drinking, find a new job, or reconcile with a marriage partner, *a written plan* will help you to stop second-, third-, and fourth-guessing your decision so you can focus primarily on achieving the goals you set.

Internal Obstacles
to Action and Growth

In a previous chapter I mentioned the destructive effects of "stinking thinking." When you examine your attitudes during times of stress or difficulty, you may often find evidence of irrational and unbiblical self-talk going on in your mind. The way you think may easily distort your views of yourself, the world, and your future. Stinking thinking patterns can block you from taking the actions necessary to recover your heart.

Depression seems to follow our descent into wrong thinking patterns, and it will likely persist unless we challenge and correct such distorted thinking. Sometimes the thinking may be so distorted or deep-seated that we need the help of a wise counselor. That, by the way, is not a sign of weakness but of personal strength. Wise women and men search out understanding; the rest suffer needlessly in their pain.

Stinking Thinking Patterns to Watch For:

+ *Black-and-white thinking*—where we view the world as all good or all bad. In reality, very few things are all good or all bad. As Christians, we can see something positive in nearly every situation.
+ *Magnification*—where we make a mountain out of a molehill.
+ *Personalization*—where we interpret someone else's behavior as a personal attack or rejection when it may not be.
+ *Catastrophizing*—when we focus on one minor negative detail while discounting the whole of a situation.
+ *Discounting the positive*—when we assert that something positive was not important while something negative was.

+ *Fortune-telling*—where we predict that key outcomes in the future are going to be negative.
+ *Emotional reasoning*—where we believe that something is true simply because we feel it is.
+ *Mind reading*—when we assume others are thinking negative things about us.
+ *Labeling*—where you label yourself as a failure, or as weak or useless.[11]

The Table of Lies Versus Truth:
How to Recognize Destructive Thinking Patterns[12]

Self-Talk (Lies)	God-Talk (Truth)
This is impossible.	With My help, all things are possible (Matt. 19:26).
I can't do this.	You can do all things with My strength (Phil. 4:13).
I'm not smart enough.	I will give you wisdom (James 1:5).
I can't forgive myself.	I forgive you (Ps. 103:12).
I can't go on.	I will strengthen and protect you (2 Thess. 3:3).
I can't manage.	I will supply all your needs (Phil. 4:19).
I'm worried.	Give your anxieties to Me, and I will give you peace (1 Pet. 5:7).
I am alone.	I will never leave you (Deut. 31:8).
Nobody loves me.	Nothing can separate you from My love (Rom. 8:38–39).

As I said earlier, we must *replace* our wrong thinking with God's thoughts about us. We begin to see our lives change when we exchange our wrong thinking about ourselves or the obstacles we face with the promises and truths God has given us in His Word.

Having made the commitment to add action to our conviction and follow through on our prescription for the restoration of heart, there is one thing remaining. We've been warned time and again by divine decree, biblical injunction, and by the advice of researchers, counselors, and friends—*don't try life alone.* We were made for relationship, and where *action* is concerned, we need the *accountability* of relationship.

We'll cover that in the pages ahead.

Questions for Discussion and Reflection

1. Have you ever had a good intention or brilliant idea that died? Why did it die? Is now the time to revive and pursue it?

2. What price is there to pay in taking action? Do you fear it? Why? What would it mean to feel the fear and do it anyway?

3. God has a way of taking the things we surrender to Him and transforming them into vehicles to lift us higher and transport us to new realms. What have you surrendered to God that He in turn used as a vehicle to transport you to new realms?

4. What spiritual disciplines come easily to you? Are you currently practicing them? What disciplines do you need to reestablish in your life? What action will you take to redeem that discipline as a part of your daily life?

5. There are five basic stages that seem to occur in our motivation process when an *action* takes place. Do you find yourself anywhere on this process (Precontemplation, Contemplation, Preparation, Action, Maintenance)?

Action Point: Be sure to apply what you've read. As you prepare to put an action plan on paper, ask the Holy Spirit to help you determine realistic yet challenging goals that will get you where you want to be spiritually, emotionally, and physically. Remember to develop both short- and long-term goals. Invite God's strength to supplement your own.

· 14 ·

ACCOUNTABLE TO WIN!

Walking Together Toward a Resurrection

The formula is simple: Mix two handfuls of troubled youth with one determined leader and an extreme challenge course too difficult and dangerous for one person to navigate alone safely. Stir briskly, permitting all the mistakes and rebellion the participants can handle, until the mixture finally blends in unity of purpose. Bake in the oven of corporate adversity until done.

This intervention recipe for at-risk kids with aggression issues has been used with success all around the country. I'm convinced our Creator invented the adversity-plus-unity recipe specifically to blend the mixed batch of "ingredients" in His house.

In His great high priestly prayer, Jesus didn't focus on defeating the enemy or providing for the needs of the saints to come. He prayed: "I do not ask in behalf of these alone, but for those also who believe in Me through their word; that they may all be one; even as You, Father, are in Me and I in You, that they also may be in Us, so that the world may believe that You sent Me" (John 17:20–21 NASB).

We are all here for a purpose. If we miss our purpose due to wrong choices, difficult circumstances, or apathy, we are not accomplishing God's plan for our lives.

How Do We Do It? *Together*

Healing is the result of a person's rising out of his pain, seeking the Father, and making sense of things in the process. Restoration is a by-product of learning how to find joy or peace in the midst of the storms of life.

How do we do it? We do it *together*.

A person on the path to healing and recovery of heart says, "Tim, I don't want to walk alone anymore. I understand it now—we were made for relationship. Man, I actually want to be around people now. I've been out there too long—it's time to engage, commit, and charge this mountain together." In *accountability*, we find connection that reminds us of—and only strengthens our bond with—the One who authors relationships. It is through accountability that we become alive again.

Today your journey looks like this:

Losing Heart: The Descent into Pain
Ambushed and Assaulted
Anger
Anxiety
Aloneness
Alienation

Arrogance
Adulteries of the Heart
Addiction
Recovery of Heart: Coming Out of Pain
Affection of God
Assessment
Awareness
Attachments
Action
Accountability

Several years ago I worked with a number of Christian leaders to produce a CD for people navigating the pain of grief. Many of the things I shared on that project also apply to people on the journey to recovery of heart. Both groups have a special need to avoid isolation and to connect with God and other caring people.

> Besides connecting with God, it's also important for us to connect with others—to share our pain with them. Grief [and pain] can, at times, cause us to feel a desire to isolate ourselves, to pull back, to avoid contact with other people. We may feel too shattered to carry on a normal conversation. We may feel irritable and impatient, or unwilling to either talk or listen. It is important to find a way to work through our craving for isolation and solitude and, at least for brief periods of time, allow others to express God's love to us.[1]

Remember Trust?

Honestly, after traveling the hard road to loss of heart with its unbroken descent into pain, you will enjoy getting to a place where you can trust somebody. Do you know what it feels like to wake up each morning knowing you don't have to fight all by yourself anymore?

✦ *Do you know what it feels like to wake up each morning knowing you don't have to fight all by yourself anymore?*

King David tells us in Psalm 68 that God personally works on behalf of the lonely, the discarded, the rejected:

A father of the fatherless and a judge for the widows,
Is God in His holy habitation.
God makes a home for the lonely;
He leads out the prisoners into prosperity,
Only the rebellious dwell in a parched land.

(Psalm 68:5–6 NASB)

Do you have an earthly friend who is this close and trusted? I'm talking about someone you trust so much that you almost brag to other people with confidence, "He's my friend. I can always count on it—that guy's gonna be there for me." "She loves me like a sister. She'll cover me!"

I sometimes wonder if David would have succeeded as he did without his best friend, Jonathan. These guys were closer than brothers—they literally risked their lives to protect one another, and they honored their commitments to each other throughout their lives.

I'm convinced that David's ability to make close friends such as Jonathan, and later, his "thirty mighty men" (2 Sam. 23), was rooted in his relationship with God. He was confident in God's love, so he inspired confidence with his own love. It was David who penned many of the great promises we claim when walking through the valley of the shadow with God.

The greatest accomplishments in life tend to be done through the *unified efforts* of many people following one leader with a single goal. David defeated Goliath in single-handed combat with God's help, but David *plus the army of Israel* defeated the army of the Philistines (1 Sam. 17:51–53).

David survived the murderous plots of King Saul in the palace with the assistance of one—his friend Jonathan or his wife, Michal. But he persevered during years of exile in the wilderness and ultimately assumed the thrones of Judah and Israel through the corporate support of thousands of soldiers and followers who gave him their loyalty (1 Sam. 19, 22:1–2; 2 Sam. 5:1–5).

King David was able to push beyond his loneliness, failure, and feelings of rejection to form strong bonds of friendship and trust with others. In a sense, even his destiny in God relied on his ability to draw others near in trusting relationships over the long haul.

In the modern era, we see the same principle in the life of the late Mother Teresa, whose compassionate care for India's rejected peoples was legendary. She could care for only one person at a time, and she often struggled to keep her ministry to the desperately poor running. But she inspired hundreds more to follow in her footsteps and managed to touch the world with her influence through loving relationships.

Surrender to and Confidence in God

The path to recovery begins and ends in surrender—the giving of ourselves to God. Yielding the power over or possession of oneself to someone else is at the heart of healing.

We surrender every day. Sometimes we surrender to peer pressure or temptation. Peter described the most important surrender in life: "Humble yourselves therefore under the mighty hand of God, that he may exalt you in due time: casting all your care upon him; for he careth for you" (1 Pet. 5:6–7 KJV). Surrender involves humility before God, submitting to His Word, His ways, and the leading of the Holy Spirit. We are to be mastered by nothing but God.

It is God Himself, our Friend, who leads us on our healing journey from brokenness to wholeness. Knowing this should produce a crescendo, a thunderous increase in our praise to Him and in our confident love for others.

This takes on immeasurable importance when you realize most people still feel at times as if they are little kids trying to make their way through a dark alley at night. Most kids aren't really afraid of the dark—they are afraid to be *alone* in the dark.

I love Paul's confidence in God when he said, "And if Christ has not been raised, your faith is worthless; you are still in your sins. . . . But now Christ has been raised from the dead, the first fruits of those who are asleep" (1 Cor. 15:17, 20 NASB). Either we believe it or we don't. We hold on to that blessed hope, that surety; and we charge the darkness, the weakness, the fears, and the failures *together* in His name. "What shall we then say to these things? If God be for us, who can be against us?" (Rom. 8:31 KJV).

Now you understand why I am so passionate about the cross, the blood, and the ministry of counseling the broken-hearted and "set[ting] at liberty them that are bruised" (Luke 4:18 KJV). If you can trust Him for heaven and eternity, you can learn to trust Him for everyday life.

If I can be a guide with the Lord on your road to recovery, then I, of all men, am most blessed.

Community: Essential to Healing

Accountability is all about connection, communion, and community. This is the environment where we thrive, where we come alive again. It is where we freely give of ourselves and enjoy the abundant fruit of lives well lived.

✦ *Accountability is all about connection,*
communion, and community.

Accountability and genuine relationship with others in Christ produce a powerful synergism, a sharing and multiplication of strength that generates breakthrough in crisis as well as in moments of weakness. In accountability, we gain the added strength and support of "Aaron and Hur" gathered around us:

Joshua did as Moses said to him, and fought with Amalek. And Moses, Aaron, and Hur went up to the top of the hill. And so it was that, when Moses held up his hand, that Israel prevailed; and when he let down his hand, Amalek prevailed. But Moses' hands became heavy; so they took a stone and put it under him, and he sat on it. And Aaron and Hur supported his hands, one on one side, and the other on the other side; and his hands were steady until the going down of the sun. So Joshua defeated Amalek and his people.

(Exodus 17:10–13)

Perhaps you've labored through life having no genuine model of what biblical relationship looks and feels like. Through no fault of your own, this lack of understanding can really hamper your pursuit of lasting and fruitful friendships.

The "love chapter" penned by the apostle Paul in 1

Corinthians 13 lists some of the most crucial attributes found in God-centered relationships empowered and governed by the Holy Spirit. This is what Paul called "a more excellent way" to live (1 Cor. 12:31):

> Though I speak with the tongues of men and of angels, but have not love, I have become sounding brass or a clanging cymbal.
>
> And though I have the gift of prophecy, and understand all mysteries and all knowledge, and though I have all faith, so that I could remove mountains, but have not love, I am nothing.
>
> And though I bestow all my goods to feed the poor, and though I give my body to be burned, but have not love, it profits me nothing.
>
> Love suffers long and is kind; love does not envy; love does not parade itself, is not puffed up; does not behave rudely, does not seek its own, is not provoked, thinks no evil; does not rejoice in iniquity, but rejoices in the truth; bears all things, believes all things, hopes all things, endures all things.
>
> Love never fails.
>
> (1 Corinthians 13:1–8)

Genuine friendship (as God ordained it) really isn't fragile. It is vibrant, dynamic, resilient, and essentially *unconditional.*

In fact, a real friend will actually challenge you and sometimes provoke you—without wrong motives or any thought of rejecting you. The Bible says, "Iron sharpeneth iron; so a man sharpeneth the countenance of his friend" (Prov. 27:17 KJV). Professional chefs often sharpen their knives by drawing them across a metal sharpener—this is a perfect picture of "iron sharpening iron."

What could you accomplish if others stood ready to uphold

your arms in prayer and practical support? Are you willing to uphold the arms of others in accountability with you? This is part of God's redemptive purpose in the life of His community.

Accountability is about intimacy, the meat and potatoes of the human soul by divine design. It's about being yoked up and bonded with what is right, not what is wrong.

Accountability isn't just a matter of checking in and saying, "Hey, did you read your Bible this week?" or "Hey, did you look at pornography?" One-dimensional, watchdog relationships of this type tend to reduce life to simple behavioral modification with no deep transformation of the heart.

Stories abound of people who walked themselves into medical center emergency rooms, complained of what seemed to be minor pain, and then passed away under the noses of the admissions nurses. In some cases, hospital staff assumed that since the persons walked in under their own power, they could survive a three-hour wait to see a physician. What the nurses did not know about was the stab wound that pierced vital organs, broken bones that had penetrated vital tissue barriers, excess fluid gathering quickly in lungs or around the heart, or internal injuries from a fall or car accident. Only a more detailed and invasive examination could reveal the hidden dangers requiring immediate intervention.

Perhaps the most difficult techniques to teach young doctors are those involving bedside manner or physician-patient interaction. In most cases, doctors learn to interpret normal, everyday symptom descriptions and translate them into more precise medical terms. This gap between medical knowledge and skilled human communication illustrates why wise doctors often rely so heavily upon the insights and communication skills of nurses, who are often more people-oriented and who often spend more personal time working with the patients and listening to what they say.

For the same reason, it is difficult to train pastors and counselors in purely academic settings. People are not automobiles, computers, or metal and plastic gadgets. They are the most incredibly complex creations God ever made. Their lives flow out of the issues of the heart.

I think the focus for accountability should be expressed in questions of the heart:

- How are you doing with God?
- Do you know how much God loves you?
- Are you free?
- Do you know His forgiveness?
- Are you crying out for mercy in that area?
- How can I help you today with that problem?

Major on the Vital Signs of the Soul

Accountability has to do with checking the vital signs of the soul rather than skimming the surface with an eye toward minor outward problems of behavior.

Vital signs reveal the state of the deeper things, the functions that keep the body alive. A person can live with a splinter or broken finger (or a smoking habit) for years if necessary, but larger issues such as a heart attack or major organ failure (or consuming pride or paralyzing fear) could bring death or tragedy within a short time if left undetected or untreated.

Pain can blind our eyes and cloud our judgment when life presses hard against the boundaries of our old comfort zones. Pain produces questions delivered with searing heat such as "Why, God?" and "Where *is* God?"

Accountability concerns matters of the heart more than actions of the body. It provides a safety net of intimate relationships rooted in unconditional love that can carry us through periods of confusion, anger, or fear and keep us from wandering back onto the path of loss of heart.

Even in their most rebellious moments, teenagers tend to realize that their parents (their chief accountability sources) deeply love them with no-strings commitment. Even when their behavior lands them in serious trouble, such as teen pregnancy, or an arrest related to drug use or alcohol, they think of Mom or Dad *first* when seeking refuge or understanding.

Why? Unconditional love is there, even if the parents also enforce strong accountability requirements. Teens know instinctively that Mom and Dad know their hearts, the true selves buried behind all of the disappointing outward behavior. This is even more true and vital in our relationship with our heavenly Father.

✦ *Accountability concerns matters of the heart*
more than actions of the body.

The late Henri Nouwen said, "Our life is full of brokenness, broken relationships, broken promises, broken expectations. How can we live with that brokenness without returning, without getting bitter and resentful, except by returning again and again to God's faithful presence in our life?"

I love that: God's *faithful* presence. He is the Foundation of our accountability safety net. It begins and ends in Him, for He is, after all, our loving God who pursues. He has moved heaven and earth to make a way for us in life's deepest sorrow, greatest disappointment, and most traumatic trial.

The Good News, the divine message of the Bible, is that God cares, and in His Son we have all we need to live beyond our circumstances and find hope. Paul the apostle mentioned a "thorn in the flesh" that he had asked God to remove. The answer he received should give all of us hope for the thorny problems in our own lives:

> For this thing I besought the Lord thrice, that it might depart from me. And he said unto me, *My grace is sufficient for thee: for my strength is made perfect in weakness.* Most gladly therefore will I rather glory in my infirmities, that the power of Christ may rest upon me. Therefore I take pleasure in infirmities, in reproaches, in necessities, in persecutions, in distresses for Christ's sake: *for when I am weak, then am I strong.*
>
> (2 Corinthians 12:8–10 KJV, emphasis mine)

And He put us *together* to make a difference in unity around the cross of Christ.

An Accountability Strategy

God provided a biblical strategy of accountability in the book of Nehemiah.[2] Here are some practical ways to incorporate accountability and help bring recovery of the heart:

Remember That You Can't Do It Alone

No wounded believer can recover by him- or herself. Yet, most feel that they should be strong enough to overcome loss of heart alone. Shame increases as the people make more and more attempts to heal in isolation. The Bible teaches that we should never undertake a long journey or complicated project alone. In Nehemiah 2, for example, the king allowed Nehemiah to go home to rebuild the wall of the city of Jerusalem, but he also sent army officers. Later, in chapter 4 of Nehemiah, the strategy is that half of the men built and half the men stood guard.

Maintain Accountability in Recovery

The key to overcoming any deep soul wound is accountability. All wounded believers need a number of people around them to provide support and encouragement.

Wounded believers should not rely on only one person to walk in accountability with them. They often begin recovery feeling as if they are alone and abandoned. If they look to only one person for relationship in accountability, they may fall back into feelings of abandonment if that one person is not available.

Wounded believers recover best when they have an accountability group of at least four or five people who really know them and whom they can call anytime. Loneliness is a major factor in soul wounds, so finding the fellowship of a group is extremely important.

Prepare in Times of Strength (The Nehemiah Principle)

Nehemiah, again in chapter 4, knew that the attack of the enemy could come at any time, and at the weakest place. He prepared for this. Wounded believers will need to prepare in their times of strength by changing their thinking and behavior for times of weakness and attack. It is not enough to wait until the attack comes. We need to make daily preparations.

All wounded believers seeking full recovery from the loss of heart should follow these simple accountability principles:

+ Never try to recover alone. Fellowship is equal to freedom from soul wounds.
+ Be in intimate accountability with at least four people.
+ Prepare in times of strength and resolve for times of attack and weakness.

We have more power when we get together! It's time to link heart to heart and start walking together. If you don't have someone to help you live according to the strategy of accountability, then ask God to bring those persons into your life now.

Perhaps the most important thing you can do to maintain maximum spiritual and mental well-being is to become anchored in a local biblical community, such as a church or small group, under a spiritual mentor. In every case, the spiritual mentors or leaders in your life should be people whom you look up to and enjoy being with because of the godly example you see in their daily lives. If you have recurring problem areas in your life (such as a substance addiction or a dysfunctional marriage relationship), it is especially helpful to have a mentor who is obviously successful and knowledgeable in that area. (And I recommend that men mentor men, and women mentor women in order to minimize the temptation. This pattern is clearly modeled in the book of Titus.)

We're coming out of the pain together. Now it's time for a resurrection of sorts: a restoration of heart and freedom is coming.

As the intimacy grows, the natural fruit is godly action bathed in accountability. Now we are on track to feel alive again.

Questions for Discussion and Reflection

1. Do you have somebody in your life, an earthly friend, who is so close and trusted that you almost brag about him or her to other people about your friendship?

2. Think back to the most difficult times in your life. You may be in such a season right now. Did you, or do you have people in your life walking with you through the muck and mire? What happens when you try to go

through the valley alone? How do you feel when you have people surrounding you in the valley? What path is easier to take?

3. How is your life defined by connection, communion, and community? What does it take to establish these aspects of accountability in your life?

4. We hear it said, "You are who you spend time with." Whom are you spending time with? Who has been around you?

5. How are you doing with God? Do you know how much He loves you? Are you free? Do you know His forgiveness? Are you crying out for mercy in any certain area of your life?

6. How can you apply the Nehemiah Principle to the weak areas of your life?

Action Point: Admit your need today of others' and God's help as you regain your heart. Thank those, in person or through a note, who helped you climb out of your pit of pain. Thank God for each one of them. Then look for someone else who might need a helping hand, and offer yours!

· 15 ·

ALIVE AGAIN!
Embracing the Dream of God for You

There's something special about coming home after a long trip. It isn't just the scruffy dog that comes to great you, or the familiar sights, smells, and oddities of the place you call home. It's everything mixed together—it's the place you've longed to reach for a thousand miles. It's where you were meant to be.

Many of us come to this place in the journey with knees that are still shaking from the trials we've endured, and hearts still tentative about risking too much too soon. But we're home.

We're *alive again*! Our broken hearts are beating with hope. And the Scripture is true: "We went through fire and through water; / But You brought us out to rich fulfillment" (Ps. 66:12).

The Lord has brought us through assault and ambush, anger

and anxiety, aloneness, alienation, and arrogance! He carried us through the painful wanderings of adulteries of the heart and delivered us from spiritual (and perhaps literal) addiction.

At last, the accuser is crushed! Some of us even feel the childlike urge to shout, "The wicked witch is dead!" By God's mercy and grace, *you've broken through to a new and better you!*

Losing Heart: The Descent into Pain
Ambushed and Assaulted
Anger
Anxiety
Aloneness
Alienation
Arrogance
Adulteries of the Heart
Addiction
Recovery of Heart: Coming Out of Pain
Affection of God
Assessment
Awareness
Attachments
Action
Accountability
Alive Again

Recent events in our lives make us even more receptive to the passages in the Apocalypse—the book of Revelation—that tell us the Dragon is doomed and the One who is called both the Lion of Judah and "the Lamb that was slain" stands center stage before the throne.

Revelation is worth reading in context at this place in the book and in our lives. This is our blessed hope, the fixed anchor upon which you and I can build our lives in total security:

And one of the elders saith unto me, Weep not: behold, the Lion of the tribe of Juda, the Root of David, hath prevailed to open the book, and to loose the seven seals thereof.

And I beheld, and, lo, in the midst of the throne and of the four beasts, and in the midst of the elders, stood a Lamb as it had been slain, having seven horns and seven eyes, which are the seven Spirits of God sent forth into all the earth.

And he came and took the book out of the right hand of him that sat upon the throne. And when he had taken the book, the four beasts and four and twenty elders fell down before the Lamb, having every one of them harps, and golden vials full of odours, which are the prayers of saints.

And they sung a new song, saying, Thou art worthy to take the book, and to open the seals thereof: for thou wast slain, and hast redeemed us to God by thy blood out of every kindred, and tongue, and people, and nation; and hast made us unto our God kings and priests: and we shall reign on the earth.

And I beheld, and I heard the voice of many angels round about the throne and the beasts and the elders: and the number of them was ten thousand times ten thousand, and thousands of thousands; saying with a loud voice, Worthy is the Lamb that was slain to receive power, and riches, and wisdom, and strength, and honour, and glory, and blessing.

And every creature which is in heaven, and on the earth, and under the earth, and such as are in the sea, and all that are in them, heard I saying, Blessing, and honour, and glory, and power, be unto him that sitteth upon the throne, and unto the Lamb for ever and ever.

(Revelation 5:5–13 KJV)

Let me say it in the vernacular of an avid sports fan: *we win!* Because Jesus won, *you and I win too!* Better than ever before, we can deeply appreciate the heavenly declaration, "They overcame [the accuser] by the blood of the Lamb and by the word of their testimony" (Rev. 12:11).

Declaring the Story of a Life Well Lived

Now we understand what is meant by "the word of their testimony." It is the story of a *life well lived*.

We echo the words of Joseph when he reassured the brothers who had sold him into slavery decades earlier: "You meant evil against me; but God meant it for good, in order to bring it about as it is this day, to save many people alive" (Gen. 50:20).

Such is God's dream for our lives, a place where the accuser is overcome and we have true purpose, meaning, and value.

✦ *Such is God's dream for our lives, a place where the accuser is overcome and we have true purpose, meaning, and value.*

In our healed lives, abundance is returning to virtually every facet, including marriage and family life, church life, ministry in the community, and favor in the workplace. We have a new appreciation for the words of Jesus: "I am come that they might have life, and that they might have it more abundantly" (John 10:10 KJV).

Once you realize that the mean dog named Satan who has been terrorizing your neighborhood for centuries is powerless because he is bound by the chain of Christ's triumph on the cross, you begin to alter the way you deal with that dog. No matter how loudly he barks, how wickedly he snarls, or how passionately he lunges toward you, you know he has been reduced to an empty threat, a rain cloud without water.

Anytime you feel oppressed by adversity, reread the back of the Book. Refresh your memory about the end game; remind yourself that *you win* in the end.

Remember how the apostle Paul put it in his letter to the Roman church: "If God be for us, who can be against us? He that spared not his own Son, but delivered him up for us all, how shall he not with him also freely give us all things?" (Romans 8:31–32 KJV).

Abundance is returning to virtually every facet of life, including marriage and family, church, ministry in the community, and favor in the workplace. We have a new appreciation for the words of Jesus: "I am come that they might have life, and that they might have it more abundantly" (John 10:10 KJV).

It's time to relax! The pressure's off. The memories of yesterday's pain are still clear, but they have lost their power to claim today. The One who freed us calls us to a *new* kind of living. John Ortberg says this life has a different type of boundary marker:

> Jesus invited people to live in the kingdom of God. Jesus invited ordinary human beings who felt they were a million miles away from God to live lives in his presence and under His power that were characterized by love and by joy and by peace. And here's the thing about Jesus: the life that He invited people to live, that's the life that Jesus lived Himself. And I believe it was Jesus' plan that that should be the case with the church.[1]

Life on This Side of the
Divide Called Brokenness

Just the fact that we are still standing puts most of us in miracle territory. It was God who drew us, God who healed us, and God who brought us back to life again.

Now we can look back at last year's memories without paralyzing pain or fear. The apostle Paul's words make more sense to us on this side of the divide called Brokenness: "For our light affliction, which is but for a moment, is working for us a far more exceeding and eternal weight of glory, while we do not look at the things which are seen, but at the things which are not seen" (2 Cor. 4:17–18).

How does the "eternal weight" of God's glory play out in your life and mine? What could God possibly do through us to affect the unseen realm or reveal His glory?

Transformation comes to your life every time you endure hard times and pain. None of us really enjoys those times, but we grow and strengthen our character more during difficult seasons.

As I mentioned earlier, my mentor once told me essentially that suffering would make me stronger and more effective in life. He was right. The person who has shed tears over a casket or who has experienced the stinging pain of betrayal or false accusation simply approaches hurting people in a different way than people who have never experienced loss or crisis. For this reason, people who have suffered and pressed through to healing and victory in life often make some of the best counselors for other hurting people.

It makes a difference when you have *experience*. Generally speaking, an experienced coach, counselor, leader, or coworker is much more effective in a painful season than those with no experience in "battle."

If I have to go through a crisis, I want the most battle-hardened and seasoned partner I can find! I'd seek out the man or woman who has been through the fire and is still standing to tell the story of God's faithfulness through the flames! I would look for someone who could say what J. I. Packer wrote in *Knowing God*: "God knows me intimately, and yet He *still* loves me!"

Welcome to the Hell-and-High-Water Crowd

Did you hear your name called just now? It was the clarion call for the Hell-and-High-Water Crowd, the company of wounded healers and scarred witnesses to the boundless love of God!

Now you have a personal testimony about the Lord's love that no one can take away, deny, or disprove. You have become a living epistle of God's love, because He loved you so patiently, persistently, and powerfully.

> ✦ *You have a personal testimony about the Lord's love that no one can take away, deny, or disprove.*

You are living Isaiah's prophecy: "The moon will shine like the sun, and the sunlight will be seven times brighter, like the light of seven full days, when the LORD binds up the bruises of his people and heals the wounds he inflicted" (Isa. 30:26 NIV).

Now that you are free and anointed to bring freedom, this is your assignment for life. You do it through *living*, not through striving. The miracle cure you carry in your heart is one you can easily tote for vast distances, and you can distribute it without limit or measure at any time, day or night.

Your gift was hard-won but freely given to you, and now you will spend the rest of your life giving it away to others: effortlessly, joyfully, without charge. And if the late Mother Teresa was right, this is the disease and evil you are commissioned to cure: "The biggest disease today is not leprosy or tuberculosis, but rather the feeling of being unwanted, uncared for, and deserted by everybody. The greatest evil is lack of love."[2]

Live Life As the Great Adventure

Now that you are alive again, life has become a great adventure. Your daily assignments have suddenly taken a turn for the better—actually for the *best*. The apostle Paul gave us a short and sweet summary of the Christian life in his letter to the Christians at Thessalonica. The task list seems short and the pomp and circumstance seem to be missing, but you are expected to pursue your duty as an adventure in intimacy and joyfulness!

Think highly of [the leaders in the Lord's work] and give them your wholehearted love because of their work. And remember to live peaceably with each other.

Brothers and sisters, we urge you to warn those who are lazy. Encourage those who are timid. Take tender care of those who are weak. Be patient with everyone.

See that no one pays back evil for evil, but always try to do good to each other and to everyone else.

Always be joyful. Keep on praying. No matter what happens, always be thankful, for this is God's will for you who belong to Christ Jesus.

Do not stifle the Holy Spirit. Do not scoff at prophecies, but test everything that is said. Hold on to what is good. Keep away from every kind of evil.

(1 Thessalonians 5:13–22 NLT)

God has strengthened you to lift the heavy burdens, so now He expects you to live the life! He heals you so that you will heal others. He raised you from the pit of despair and left the rope with you, assuming you know what to do with it.

The Bible spells it out in 2 Corinthians: "Blessed be the God and Father of our Lord Jesus Christ, the Father of mercies and God of all comfort, who comforts us in all our affliction so that we may be able to comfort those who are in any affliction *with the comfort with which we ourselves are comforted* by God" (2 Cor. 1:3–4 NASB, emphasis mine).

God leads us from despair to salvation and wholeness so that we can lead others from despair to salvation and wholeness through Christ as well!

✦ *He raised you from the pit of despair*
and left the rope with you.

With the world changing so quickly, God's army of healers, encouragers, and overcomers automatically begin, by His Spirit, to reach hurting people with Jesus' love. This puts a premium value on those who know what it means to be healed and made whole. Taken together, we are all called to spread the Good News through our truly transformed lives around the world.

This is nothing to stress out about. It is the greatest opportunity in human history to see the lost saved, the broken healed, and the fallen restored! Whom has God chosen to deliver His cure to the hurting? And what hope will be offered to them? Larry Crabb and Dan Allender penned these words: "So what is our hope? Simply this: That nothing, no problem in our circumstances or in our souls, can keep us from living out God's purpose for our lives if we are abandoned to Him."[3]

Who will lead those who are descending into pain and losing heart on the journey back to the recovery of heart?

It must be someone who knows the way, someone who has been there and still lives to tell the story.

The story goes that when Disney World first opened in Florida shortly after the death of Walt Disney, someone remarked to a park designer, "It is sad that Mr. Disney did not live to see this." "Oh, but he did see it," replied the designer. "That's why the park is here."

"Oh, but He did see it," replied the scarred healer.
"That's why I am still here despite all of the sorrows and adversities."

Dear reader, please know my prayer for you. Hope is yours, and you can turn your life around. You can realize God's dream just for you. You know He has been whispering your name and carrying you along the way. Why? Because He loves you and wants you—yes, *you*—to be free.

Questions for Discussion and Reflection

1. When you are feeling oppressed, what do you do to overcome these feelings? Allow me to challenge you to read the back of the Book. Refresh your memory of the end game; remind yourself that *you win* in the end.

2. Read Galatians 5:1. What does this verse mean to you? What does it mean to be free and living in abundance?
3. How has God used suffering in your life to build character? How have you become more like Him in your sufferings? Do you find it easier to help others in similar circumstances?
4. Read 1 Thessalonians 5:13–22. How can you incorporate these aspects of the Christian life into your character and daily habits?

Action Point: Congratulations! You have ascended out of the pain and into health and joy. What will you do with your new life? Determine now whom you will turn to, what safeguards you will employ, when deep pain or disappointment assails you in the future. Then go, and embrace the adventures God has designed for you!

AUTHOR'S NOTE

Dear Reader,

If after reading this book you still find yourself struggling with pain, discouragement, or bouts of depression; if you find that you are not breaking free from past patterns that held you in bondage, talk with your pastor, consult with a Christian counselor, or contact the offices of the American Association of Christian Counselors at 1-800-526-8673 or visit www.AACC.net. We will be happy to help refer you to a qualified Christ-centered counselor in your area.

The American Association of Christian Counselors is an association of nearly fifty thousand professional counselors, pastors, and lay leaders. These are people committed to biblical integrity and clinical excellence in Christian counseling and to assisting members in the development of their own counseling practices.

The AACC exists to bring honor to Jesus Christ; to encourage and promote excellence in counseling worldwide; to disseminate information, educational resources, and counseling aids; to inspire the highest levels of counselor training; and to contribute to the strengthening of families.

I pray you will find the healing you need and desire.

—Tim Clinton
TimClinton.com

NOTES

Chapter 1: Ambushed and Assaulted

1. Bruce Wilkinson, *The Dream Giver* (Sisters, OR: Multnomah Publishers, 2003).

2. The Barna Group, "Born Again Christians Just as Likely to Divorce as Non-Christians," *The Barna Update*, September 8, 2004, http://www.barna.org/FlexPage.aspx?Page=BarnaUpdate&BarnaUpdateID=170; (accessed May 2005)

3. Rebecca O'Neill, *Experiments in Living: The Fatherless Family*, http://www.civitas.org.uk/pubs/experiments.php?PHPSESSID=04a55719634 43f82281d8c0bd4332322#Results: The Institute for the Study of Civil Society, September 2002 (accessed June 2005).

4. The National Center for Fathering, *The Consequences of Fatherlessness*, http://www.fathers.com/research/consequences.html (accessed May 20, 2005).

5. Alfred Ells, "Leaders Need Other Leaders," *Pastor's Family Edition of Focus on the Family* magazine (December 2002). http://www.family.org/pastor/pfministry/a0024693.cfm (accessed February 20, 2006).

6. George Barna, *The Index of Leading Spiritual Indicators* (Nashville, TN: Thomas Nelson Publishers, 1996).

Chapter 2: Anger: The Fiery Furnace of the Soul

1. Gary J. Oliver, "Cultivating Healthy Anger," *The Soul Care Bible*, exec. ed. Tim Clinton (Nashville: Thomas Nelson Publishers, 2001), 692.

2. Gary Oliver, *Real Men Have Feelings Too* (Chicago: Moody Press, 1993). There is some controversy among counseling professionals and researchers over whether anger is a primary emotion or a secondary emotion. This question is beyond the scope and purpose of this book, so we present Dr. Oliver's professional conclusion as is.

3. Gary R. Oliver and Carrier E. Oliver, "Managing Your Anger and Making It Work for You," *Caring for People God's Way*, ed. Tim Clinton, Archibald Hart, and George Ohlschlager (Nashville: Thomas Nelson, Inc., 2005), 204–205.

4. Dan B. Allender, PhD, *The Healing Path: How the Hurts in Your Past Can Lead You to a More Abundant Life* (Colorado Springs, CO: WaterBrook Press, 1999), 62.

5. Ibid, 63–64.

6. Rick Renner, *Sparkling Gems from the Greek: 365 Greek Word Studies for Every Day of the Year to Sharpen Your Understanding of God's Word* (Tulsa: Teach All Nations, a division of Rick Renner Ministries, 2003), 839.

7. Dr. Neil Clark Warren, interview with the author, "Anger Management." Produced and distributed by American Association of Christian Counselors (AACC).

8. Gary R. Oliver and H. Norman Wright, *When Anger Hits Home* (Chicago: Moody Press, 1992).

9. Neil Clark Warren, PhD, *Make Anger Your Ally*, 3rd ed. (Wheaton, IL: Tyndale House, 1999). Dr. Warren's career as a clinical psychologist spans thirty-five years, and after "presiding over the funerals of hundreds of marriages," as he puts it, he began an in-depth study of why marriages fail. This body of work produced nine bestselling books on relationship success and led to the founding of e-Harmony.com, a nationally recognized relationship-building service designed to strengthen relationships and transform marriages.

10. Clinton, Hart, and Ohlschlager, *Caring for People*, 208–213, adapted.

11. James Strong, *Strong's Exhaustive Concordance of the Bible* (Peabody, MA: Hendrickson Publishers, n.d.), "double minded," Greek 5590, *dipsuchos*.

12. Richard Walters, *Anger: Yours & Mine & What to Do About It* (Grand Rapids: Zondervan Publishers, 1981).

Chapter 3: Anxious and Barely Holding On

1. Archibald Hart and Catherine Hart Weber, "Stress and Anxiety" in Clinton, Hart, and Ohlschlager, *Caring for People*, 164; Susan M. Lark, *Anxiety and Stress* (Berkley, CA: Celestialarts, 1996), 10; and Richard A. Swensen, *Margin* (Colorado Springs, CO: NavPress, 1995), 20.

2. Hart and Weber, "Stress and Anxiety," 164, 162.

3. Dr. Larry Crabb and Dr. Dan Allender, *Hope When You're Hurting* (Grand Rapids: Zondervan Publishing House, 1996), 22–23.

4. John Ortberg, PhD, "The Life You've Always Wanted" (lecture, AACC World Conference, Forest, VA, 2001). I strongly recommend Dr. Ortberg's book in which he greatly expands upon the principles, stories, and points of this lecture: *The Life You've Always Wanted: Spiritual Disciplines for Ordinary People* (Grand Rapids: Zondervan Publishing House, 1997).

5. Ibid.

6. Ibid.

7. Hart and Weber, "Stress and Anxiety," 166–168.

8. *Merriam Webster's Collegiate Dictionary*, 10th ed. (Springfield, MA: Merriam-Webster, Inc., 1997), 53, adapted from etymologies and definitions for "anxious" and "anxiety."

9. Christine Gorman, "The Science of Anxiety," *Time*, June 10, 2002, 46.

10. For more details, see the table, "Symptoms of General Stress and Anxiety" and other helpful information in Hart and Weber, "Stress and Anxiety," 166.

11. *Merriam Webster's Collegiate Dictionary*, "trauma," definition 1b, 1257.

12. Nikki N. Jordan, C. W. Hoge, S. K. Tobler, J. Wells, G. J. Dydek, and W. E. Egerton, "Mental Health Impact of 9/11 Pentagon Attack: Validation of a Rapid Assessment Tool," *American Journal of Preventive Medicine* 26 (April 2004): 284–294.

13. Nancy Fagan and K. Freme, "Confronting Posttraumatic Stress Disorder," *Nursing* 34 (February 2004): 52–54; Dr. Tim Clinton, *Reliving Trauma: Post-Traumatic Stress Disorder: A Brief Overview of the Symptoms, Treatments, and Research Findings* (Washington, D.C.: National Institute of Mental Health, 2001).

14. Eldra P. Solomon and K. M. Heide, "The Biology of Trauma," *Journal of Interpersonal Violence* 20 (January 2005): 51–61; Thomas A. Mellman and D. David, "Sleep Disturbance and Its Relationship to Psychiatric Morbidity after Hurricane Andrew," *American Journal of Psychiatry* 152 (November 1995): 1659–1664; Jean M. Thomas, "Traumatic Stress Disorder Presents as Hyperactivity and Disruptive Behavior: Case Presentation, Diagnoses, and Treatment," *Infant Mental Health Journal* 16 (Winter 1995): 306–318; Kathy A. Perce, A. H. Schauer, N. J. Garfield, C. O. Ohlde, and T. W. Patterson, "A Study of Post Traumatic Stress Disorder in Vietnam Veterans," *Journal of Clinical Psychology* 41 (January 1985): 9–15.

15. Marcelle Farrada-Noli, M. Asberg, K. Ormstad, T. Lundin and E. Sundbom, "Suicidal Behavior After Severe Trauma. Part 1: PTSD Diagnoses, Psychiatric Comorbidity, and Assessments of Suicidal Behavior," *Journal of Traumatic Stress* 11 (January 1998): 103–113; Rani A. Desai, D. J. Dausey and R. Rosenheck, "Mental Health Service Directory and Suicide Risk: The Role of Individual Patient and Facility Factors," *American Journal of Psychiatry* 162 (February 2005), 311–319.

Chapter 4: Alone and Wounded in an Uncaring World

1. Meditation XVII from "Devotions upon Emergent Occasions" by John Donne.

2. Donald Miller, *Blue Like Jazz* (Nashville, TN: Thomas Nelson Publishers, 2003).

3. American Association of Suicidology, Elderly Suicide Fact Sheet, http://www.211bigbend.org/hotlines/suicide/SuicideandtheElderly.pdf (accessed March 14, 2006).

4. *The AACC Bible Counseling Guide* (not yet published), AACC 1st pages-Topics36-40.indd, 22–27. Hereafter referred to as *AACC Guide*.

Chapter 5: Cruising on Alienation Highway

1. Allender, *Healing Path*, 25.

2. C. S. Lewis, *The Great Divorce: A Dream* (San Francisco: HarperSanFrancisco, 2001), 9–10.

3. Ibid., 11–12.

4. Beth Moore, *When Godly People Do Ungodly Things: Arming Yourself in the Age of Seduction* (Nashville, TN: Lifeway Christian Resources, 2003).

Chapter 6: Arrogance on Parade

1. Dr. Charles Stanley, *The Power of the Cross* (Nashville: Thomas Nelson Publishers, 1998), 169.

2. John Eldredge, *Wild at Heart* (Nashville, TN: Thomas Nelson Publishers, 2001), 110.

3. Archibald D. Hart and Catherine H. Weber, *Unveiling Depression in Women: A Practical Guide to Understanding and Overcoming Depression* (Grand Rapids: Fleming H. Revell, 2002), 23.

4. Ibid.

5. Margaret Strock, et al., "Depression," National Institute of Health Publication No. 00-3561 (2000), http://www.nimh.nih.gov/publicat/depression.cfm (accessed February 25, 2003).

Chapter 7: Adulteries of the Heart

1. C. S. Lewis, *The Problem of Pain* (New York: MacMillan Publishing Co., Inc., 1977), 96.

2. Clinton, Hart, and Ohlschlager, *Caring for People*.

3. *AACC Guide*, AACC 1st pages-Topics26-30.indd, "Pornography," pp. 22–29, citing data posted by Familysafemedia.com.

4. "The Leadership Journal Survey on Pastors and Internet Pornography," *Leadership Journal*, Spring 2001.

5. David Ljunggren, "Canadian Court Allows Clubs for Group Sex," Reuters, December 21, 2005, http://news.yahoo.com/s/nm/20051221/wl_canada_nm/canada_sex.

6. Ernest Becker, *The Denial of Death* (New York: The Free Press, 1973).

Chapter 8: Addiction: Embracing the Gods of Distraction

1. Gerald May, *Addiction & Grace* (San Francisco: HarperSanFrancisco, 1991).

2. Dallas Willard, *The Divine Conspiracy: Rediscovering Our Hidden Life in God* (New York: HarperCollins, 1998).

3. *AACC Guide*, AACC "Third Pages" Topic010205.indd, "Addictions," pp. 8–9; 9-27-2005. Adapted from sections titled in the original document, "Definitions and Key Thoughts" and "Character of Addiction" respectively.

4. Lewis, *Problem of Pain*, 115.

5. James Dobson, *When God Doesn't Make Sense* (Wheaton, IL: Tyndale Publishers, 1993), 20.

6. Ortberg, "The Life You've Always Wanted."

7. Ibid.

8. Lewis, *Problem of Pain*, 95–96.

9. George MacDonald, *Unspoken Sermons. First Series*. It is with this quote that C. S. Lewis chose to open his classic book *The Problem of Pain*.

Chapter 9: The Affection of the Pursuing God

1. Lewis, *Problem of Pain*, 111.

2. Philip Yancey, *Where Is God When It Hurts?* (Grand Rapids, MI: Zondervan Publishers, 1990), 62.

3. This doesn't give us permission to favor the bar over the church—His love burns but His justice remains. A parent's love for his child burns brightly all the way up to the prison gate and even through the execution chamber. We all must give account for our sin, but even those who refuse to turn and end up in hell will go there with God's love burning for them.

4. Os Guiness, *The Long Journey Home* (Colorado Springs, CO: Waterbrook Press, 2001).

5. Lewis, *Problem of Pain*, 97.

6. Ibid.

7. Ortberg, *The Life You've Always Wanted* (Grand Rapids: Zondervan, 1997), 208.

8. Marsha Gallardo, "The Secret of Genuine Praise," *Charisma*, January 2006, 37.

9. Joni Eareckson Tada, interview with the author, *Helping You to Live the Life*, Spirit FM.

10. Yancey, *Where Is God*, 18.

Chapter 10: Exposed to Love and Assessing Our Mess

1. Allender, *Healing Path*, 213.

2. Lewis, *Great Divorce*, 75.

3. Dr. Tim Clinton and Dr. Gary Sibcy, *Why You Do the Things You Do* (Nashville, TN: Integrity Publishers, 2002), 43–44.

4. Ibid.

5. Ortberg, "The Life You've Always Wanted."

Chapter 11: Finally Aware of the Great Desire

1. Richard Foster, *The Celebration of Discipline: The Path to Spiritual Growth* (New York: HarperCollins, 1978).

2. Ortberg, "The Life You've Always Wanted."

3. Eldredge, *Wild at Heart*, 111–112.

4. Allender, *Healing Path*, 212.

Chapter 12: Attached and Thriving

1. Clinton and Sibcy, *Why You Do*, 152–154.

2. Ibid., 147.

3. Ibid., 151.

4. Ibid., 149.

5. Ibid., 148.

6. Ibid., 173.

7. Ibid., 157–158.

8. A. W. Tozer, *The Pursuit of God* (1949).

9. Crabb and Allender, *Hope When You're Hurting*, 117.

10. Ibid., 201.

11. Clinton and Sibcy, *Why You Do*, 175.

12. Dr. Gary Smalley, *The DNA of Relationships* (Wheaton, IL: Tyndale House Publishers, Inc., 2004), 37.

13. Frank Parsons, interview with the author, *Helping You to Live the Life*, Spirit FM.

14. Allender, *Healing Path*, 213.

15. Ortberg, "The Life You've Always Wanted."

Chapter 13: Action Required

1. Bishop T. D. Jakes (lecture, "Live the Life" AACC World Conference, Nashville, TN, 2003).

2. Lewis, *Great Divorce*, 106.

3. Ibid.

4. Ortberg, "The Life You've Always Wanted."

5. Clinton and Sibcy, *Why You Do*, 163–171.

6. Jakes, "Live the Life" conference.

7. Everett L. Worthington Jr. and Jennifer S. Ripley, "Christian Marriage and Marital Counseling: Promoting Hope in Lifelong Communities," *Competent Christian Counseling*, vol. 1, *Foundations and Practice of Compassionate Soul Care*, ed. Dr. Timothy Clinton and Dr. George Ohlschlager (Colorado Springs, CO: Waterbrook Press, 2002), 467.

8. Warren, "Anger Management."

9. Clinton and Ohlschlager, *Caring for People*, 24.

10. G. Egan, *The Skilled Helper: A Problem-Management Approach to Helping*, 6th ed. (Pacific Grove, CA: Brooks/Cole, 1998), 306.

11. David D. Burns, *The Feeling Good Handbook* (New York: Plume, 1999).

12. Adapted from a list reproduced by Henry A. Virkler, "Personality Disorders" in Clinton and Ohlschlager, *Caring for People*, 237. I made considerable changes in titles, sections, and order, and I added Scripture references.

Chapter 14: Accountable to Win!

1. Dr. Tim Clinton et al., *A Healing Journey Through Grief*, (Costa Mesa, CA: Maranatha! Music, 2003).

2. Clinton, Hart, and Ohlschlager, *Caring for People*, 262–263, adapted.

Chapter 15: Alive Again!

1. Ortberg, "The Life You've Always Wanted."

2. Clinton and Sibcy, *Why You Do*, 75.

3. Crabb and Allender, *Hope When You're Hurting*, 203–204.